THE
FROG
BOOK
RUSSELL ASH

Macdonald
Queen Anne Press

A *Queen Anne Press* BOOK

© Russell Ash 1986

First published in Great Britain in 1986 by
Queen Anne Press, a division of
Macdonald & Co (Publishers) Ltd
3rd Floor
Greater London House
Hampstead Road
London NW1 7QX

A BPCC plc Company

Cover illustrations: *Helen Vicat*
Cover design: *Clare Forte*

British Library Cataloguing in Publication Data

Ash, Russell
    The frog book.
    I. Title
    828'.91409   PN6175

    ISBN 0 356 12305 7

Typeset by Leaper & Gard Limited, Bristol

Printed and bound in Great Britain by
Hazell, Watson & Viney Limited, Aylesbury, Bucks

A Member of the BPCC Group

PICTURE CREDITS

Ardea: 13R.
Biofotos: 12, 17L, 21.
BPCC: 10, 13L, 23 & 24 © Marlboro House
    1950, 32, 33L, 37, 40, 42, 48, 49, 55, 60L, 61,
    68, 70R, 74, 75R, 76, 78, 80, 82, 84, 88.
BPCC, photo Angelo Hornak, Courtesy of
    the Dolls House Toy Museum, Arundel: 8,
    31, 71, 83R, 86, 87.
British Library: 75L, *Harl 4431, 105V.*
Collection of Richard Dennis, Esq: 85R.
© Don Dougherty 1982 from *Croakers,* Corgi
    Books 1983: 16, 19, 30, 46L, 62, 69.
Mary Evans Picture Library: 7, 44, 63, 66,
    70L; 72, 79R, 81 © Mrs Barbara Edwards.
Fortean Picture Library: 45 © Fate
    Magazine, 46R, 53, 59.
Göteborg Etnografiska Museum: 58.
Haags Gemeentemuseum: 79L © Cordon
    Art BV.
Michael Holford: 28 © Robin Gwynn, 57,
    60R.
Kelsey Museum of Archaeology, Michigan:
    38.
David King Collection: 85L.
© Albert Lobel 1970, from *Frog and Toad are
    Friends,* Puffin Books 1983: 64.
Mansell Collection: 27, 29, 33R, 34.
MAS: 39 Museum del Prado.
NHPA: 17R, 89.
Rex: 26.
Brian Shuel: 83L.

CONTENTS

'BE KIND AND TENDER TO THE FROG'

Be kind and tender to the Frog,
And do not call him names,
As 'Slimy skin' or 'Polly-wog',
Or likewise 'Ugly James',
Or 'Gap-a-grin', or 'Toad-gone-wrong,'
Or 'Bill Bandy-knees':
The Frog is justly sensitive
To epithets like these.
No animal will more repay
A treatment kind and fair;
At least so lonely people say
Who keep a frog (and, by the way,
They are extremely rare).

[HILAIRE BELLOC, 'THE FROG', FROM
A BAD CHILD'S BOOK OF BEASTS, 1896]

The frog by nature is both damp and
   cold,
Her mouth is large, her belly much will
   hold.

[JOHN BUNYAN, *A BOOK FOR BOYS AND GIRLS*,
1686]

Few creatures excite such mixed emotions as the frog and toad. The Swedish scientist, Linnaeus (1707-78), was no frog-lover, writing: 'These foul and loathsome animals ... are abhorent because of their cold bodies, pale colour, cartilaginous skeletons, filthy skins, fierce aspect, calculating eye, offensive smell, harsh voices, squalid habitation and terrible venom.' But then, Linnaeus was a botanist!

Many dismiss them as nasty, slimy creatures — poisonous, even — while in the

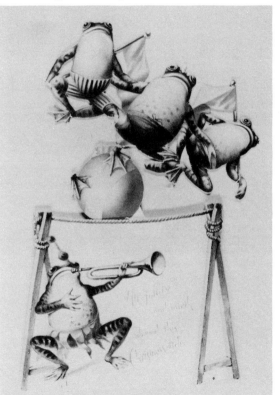

A far croak from the 'loathsome' frog — acrobatic frogs on a Christmas card.

Toads take to the road — a couple of elegant Edwardian ceramic motorists.

vocabulary of abuse, calling a Frenchman 'Froggy' or anyone a toad will not win you many friends. Yet for centuries these same animals have also been worshipped and revered in myths and legends and endearingly featured in all forms of popular culture. In modern times they have appeared as lovable children's characters, such as Beatrix Potter's Mr Jeremy Fisher and Kenneth Grahame's Toad of Toad Hall, as a television megastar in the internationally adored form of Kermit the Muppet, as a family of cartoon frogs in Paul McCartney's film, *Rupert and the Frog Song*, and as an affectionate motif in a vast and growing array of froggy greetings cards and ornaments.

Why are they despised, yet avidly collected in a multitude of inanimate forms? Why do we have such ambivalent feelings about frogs and toads? In the following pages this question is answered in a wide-ranging examination of the frog itself and its unique role in our culture — its surprising value to mankind, its significance in magic and myth, literature, art, in world cuisine and in our language.

THE PRIVATE LIFE OF THE FROG AND TOAD

Today as I went out to play
I saw a brown frog in the way,
I know that frogs are smooth and green,
But this was brown — what could it mean?
I asked a lady in the road;
She said it was a spotted toad!

[MARY K. ROBINSON, 'THE BROWN FROG']

It is not always easy to distinguish between frogs and toads. Britain happens to have few examples of either, and the differences are fairly obvious, but elsewhere in the world the distinctions are more subtle, and even herpetologists (specialists in the study of reptiles and amphibians — from the Greek, *herpeton*, a creeping animal) are often hard-pressed to say whether a particular creature is a frog or a toad. Also, because the word 'frog,' applies to the entire order, as well as the genus, *Rana* (which means literally 'voice'), all toads are frogs, but not all frogs are toads!

Frogs and toads are both amphibians. 'Amphibian' means 'double life,' and refers to the fact that such creatures can live either in water or on the land, though they may be better adapted to spend most of their lives in one or the other environment.

There are three groups of such animals: the lowest order is *Gymnophiona* (legless, subterranean worm-like animals); then comes *Caudata* (the salamanders); finally *Salienta*, which comprises frogs and toads, of which there are more than 2,600 different species, with new ones being discovered all the time.

Amphibians have a distinct advantage that aids their survival: they can escape from terrestrial predators by jumping into the water, and from aquatic attackers by leaping onto the land. Added to this, many types are capable of producing poisonous substances in their skins, which reduces the number of enemies prepared to tackle them. They are most vulnerable at the stage between egg and adult, and the huge quantity of eggs produced by most frogs is based on the expectation that it is unlikely that all will be eaten by predators. Toads usually lay more eggs than frogs — perhaps up to 10,000 at a time, and all sorts of ingenious adaptations ensure the protection of the young of those species that produce relatively few eggs.

Frogs are found virtually everywhere in the world, except where the ground is permanently frozen, and in marine areas (despite the fact that one of the commonest of all is misleadingly called the Marine toad, they seldom live anywhere near the sea). Not all frogs live in water, however; the greatest variety occurs in the tropical rainforests, and some are completely adapted to spending their entire lives as tree-dwellers, while others are found in desert conditions.

Neither frogs nor toads are particularly intelligent, but toads are probably more intelligent than frogs: toads can learn their way round a maze more quickly than frogs — frogs tend to bash their heads repeatedly on glass partitions, while toads soon learn

A leggy Phyllomedusa *tree frog, from a German natural history book of 1863.*

not to. If you put a toad on the edge of a table, it will peer over and estimate the distance, and if it is too high will refuse to jump; frogs just leap off regardless in a kamikaze dive. Toads remember regular feeding times, and learn quickly to refuse inedible foodstuffs. They can be easily tamed, respond if called and like to be petted. There are many instances of frogs and toads being 'adopted' by humans: Gilbert White, the author of *The Natural History of Selborne*, described in a letter of 18 June 1768 how '... some ladies (ladies you will say of peculiar taste) took a fancy to a toad'. They fed it until it '... grew to a monstrous size'. He reported that 'The reptile used to come forth every evening from a hole under the garden steps; and was taken up, after supper, on the table to be fed.'

FROG FACTS

Underneath the water-weeds
Small and black, I wriggle,
And life is most surprising!
Wiggle! Waggle! Wiggle!
There's every now and then a most
Exciting change in me,
I wonder, wiggle! waggle!
What I *shall* turn out to be!

[E.E. GOULD, *THE TADPOLE*]

The male Red-eyed tree frog, *Agalychnis callidryas*, is half the size of the female, but her egg cluster is bigger than both of them.

The Dagger frog, *Babina holsti*, found in Okinawa, has a sharp spiny 'thumb' which it uses to stab anyone foolish enough to pick it up.

African male Hairy frogs, *Astylosternus robustus*, actually have hairlike filaments on their sides and thighs during the breeding season. These probably play a part in supplying extra oxygen intake at this time when their metabolic rate is high.

African *Breviceps* toads cannot swim, and lay their eggs on land.

Some fossil amphibians had a third eye, the so-called 'pineal eye'. Vestiges of this are still visible in some tadpoles and frogs.

The European Spadefoot toad, *Pelobates fuscus*, exudes a garlic-like secretion, and is thus known in Germany as the 'Knoblauchskröte,' or garlic toad.

The larva of the Paradoxical frog, *Pseudis paradoxa*, of Trinidad and the Amazon, which can be up to ten inches long, are much bigger than the frogs they turn into, which average around three inches — which is somewhat paradoxical.

Some frogs, such as the African Lesser banana frog, *Megalixalus stuhlmanni*, occasionally have such transparent flesh that their limb bones are visible through it.

Malayan Flying frogs, *Rhacophorus rein-wardtii*, are skilled at leaping among trees, but they cannot fly.

The White-lipped frog, found in the Puerto Rican rain forest, was recently discovered to communicate by thumping the ground with its throat pouch. This can be detected by other frogs up to eighteen feet away.

The South African Arum frog, *Hyperolius horstockii*, resides in the centre of a water lily while it is in bloom, living on insects attracted to the flower.

Oreophrynella quelchii is found in only one place in the world, Mount Roraima in British Guiana.

The tailed frog, *Ascaphus truei*, does not have a tail.

A Costa Rican flying frog.

THE EDIBLE FROG

Most frogs and toads are theoretically edible, but some are simply too small to be worth the effort. The so-called Edible frog, *Rana esculenta*, a gourmet dish since Roman times, is said to have been imported into eastern England — Cambridge and the Fen Country — by a Mr Berney in the 1830s and '40s. He started with 1,500 frogs plus their spawn, and their ancestors can still be found.

UNDESIRABLE ALIENS

In the 1940s, African clawed frogs, *Xenopus laevis*, were imported into the United States for medical experiments, including pregnancy testing. It was soon discovered that indigenous frogs were just as useful, and laboratory animals were set free into the wild. They have since invaded southern Californian rivers and have become a serious ecological problem. They are very vicious, have no natural enemies and are rapid breeders; they have virtually destroyed the local stickleback population.

FROG NAMES

Many frogs have strange or attractive common and scientific names, for example:

Catholic frog	*Notaden bennetti*
Cricket frog	*Acris gryllus gryllus*
Fire-bellied toad	*Bombina bombina*
Meadow frog	*Rana pipiens pipiens*

Acris gryllus, *the cricket frog.*

Mountain chorus frog	*Pseudacris brachyphora*
Oregon red-legged frog	*Rana aurora aurora*
Peeper	*Hyla crucifer crucifer*
Texan cliff frog	*Eleutherodactylus latrans*
Warty frog	*Rana tuberculosa*

PECULIAR PARENTS

'The frog saith Aristotle liveth quietly all the time in cold weather, and never stireth above, until time of coite or coniunation [mating]. And then by croking voice he allureth the Female and stireth her to Venerie.'

The pouch-backed Marsupial frog.

[JOHN MAPLET, *A GREENE FOREST, OR A NATURALL HISTORIE,* 1567]

The Surinam toad, *Pipa pipa,* lays about sixty eggs, which are then manoeuvred onto the female's back where they develop in tiny pockets; fully developed baby toads, or toad-lets, emerge, without tails or gills. The Marsupial frog, *Gastrotheca marsupiata,* has a similar life cycle: tiny young escape from pouches on the female's back.

The Fire-bellied toad, *Bombina bombina,* attaches its eggs to the undersides of stones.

Nectaphrynoides, found in Africa, bears live young — up to a hundred at a birth.

Rohde's treefrog, *Phyllomedusa rohdei*, glues eggs to leaves overhanging the water; when the tadpoles develop, they drop off and swim away.

The *Dendrobates* Strawberry frog lays only two eggs. The tadpoles cling to the female's back and are deposited into water in bromeliad plants. The thoughtful female lays additional, but infertile, eggs to feed the young tadpoles.

As recently as 1984, the so-called platypus frog, *Rheobatrachus silus*, formerly thought to be extinct, was discovered in Queensland, Australia. It is unusual in that the female swallows the eggs and releases the young from her mouth; they spend their entire lives in water, making it the only totally aquatic frog.

MALE BABY-SITTERS

The males of certain frogs take an unusual interest in caring for their offspring. Even before it acquires a mate, the male Chinese *Rana adenopleura* builds a nest on the river or pond bank. The male Midwife toad, *Alytes obstetricans*, gathers up fertilised eggs and keeps them attached to his body for about a month. While they are developing, the eggs of the Barking frog, *Eleutherodactylus latrans*, are protected by the male. Tadpoles of the Two-toned arrow-poison frog, *Phyllobates bicolor*, of Peru fix themselves to the father's back. The male Mouth-breeding or

Darwin's frog (so-named because it was discovered in South America by Charles Darwin), *Rhinoderma darwinii*, retains fertilised eggs (not necessarily those he has fertilised) in his vocal sac, spitting them out when they turn into tadpoles.

FROG SOUNDS

Can these, indeed, be voices, that so greet
The twilight still? I seem to hear
Oboe and cymbal in a rhythmic beat
With bass-drum and bassoon; their drear
And dull crescendo, louder growing,
Then falling back, like waters ebbing, flowing,—
Back to the silence sweet!

[FLORENCE EARLE COATES *THE FROGS*]

Quaint and low, like some remote bassoon
Across the marsh there came a muffled croon,
And all alone one melancholy frog,
Squat on the butt of a sunken log,
Solemnly did serenade the Moon:—
In tone so low and quaint — like the quaint bassoon.

[FROM TOM MACINNES (CANADIAN POET), *THE MOONLIT WHEAT*, 1923]

The Toads' choir will never tire
aspiring to give delight.
Koak, Koak, croaketty, croak,
every note is right.

I and all the other fellows in our cravats
of bilious yellow
Clog, grog, sit on a log, sing on a log all
night.
Brekekekekekekek. This is our
quarterdeck.
Lumpkin, Bumpkin, Mumkin, Tumpkin,
Pumpkin nightly cry.
Brekekekekekek. Swell our stomach
and neck.
Odkin, Bodkin, Didkin, Pod and I.
Eyes host to a sadness ghost,
mouth that is post-box wide.
Quick, lick, licketty click,
insects are flicked inside.
Skin in folds and wrinkled, crinkled,
clammy cold and spot besprinkled.
Ugh! Glug! Slimed as a slug, slimed as a
slug our tribe.
Brekekekekek. All on our quarterdeck.
Muffin, Stuffin, Huffin, Chuffin, Puffin
nightly cry.
Jerkin, Perkin, Firkin, Ghurk and I
Call us hideous
venomous its a lie.
We spurt a villainous squirt
only would hurt a fly.
I and all the other fellows work our
cheeks and throats like bellows.
Brekekekekek. Brekekekekek
Stop! Hop! Flippety flip!
Plop-plop-plop-plop!
Goodbye!

[RUMER GODDEN, *THE TOADS' CHORUS*]

The poetic nature of toad sounds was described by William Henry Hudson in his *The Book of a Naturalist* (1919) in his description of the spring mating season:

They arrive single and are in hundreds, a gathering of hermits from the desert places, drunk with excitement, and filling the place with noise and commotion. A strange sound, when at intervals the leader or precentor or bandmaster for the moment blows himself out into a wind instrument — a fairy bassoon, let us say, with a tremble to it — and no sooner does he begin than a hundred more join in; and the sound, which the scientific books describe as 'croaking,' floats far and wide, and produces a beautiful, mysterious effect on a still evening when the last heavy-footed labourer has trudged home to his tea, leaving the world to darkness and to me.

As I sat in the rain a little tree-frog, about half-an-inch long, leaped on to a grassy leaf, and began a tune as loud as that of many birds, and very sweet; it was surprising to hear so much music out of so small a musician.

[DAVID LIVINGSTONE, *LAST JOURNALS*, 1874]

In 1845, on a trip to Germany, the British naturalist Frank Buckland captured a dozen green tree frogs, notable for their noisy croaking, in the woods of Giessen:

I started at night on my homeward journey by the diligence [carriage], and I put the bottle containing the frogs into the pocket inside the diligence. My fellow passengers were sleepy old smoke-dried Germans. Very little conversation took place, and, after the first mile, every one settled himself to sleep, and soon all were snoring. I suddenly awoke with a start, and found all the sleepers had been roused at the same moment. On their sleepy faces were depicted fear and anger. What had woke us up so suddenly? The morning was just breaking, and my frogs, though in the dark pocket of the coach, had found it out, and, with one accord, all twelve of them had begun their morning song. As if at a given signal, they one and all of them began to croak as hard as ever they could. The noise their united concert made, seemed, in the closed compartment of the coach, quite deafening: well might the Germans look angry; they wanted to throw the frogs, bottle and all, out of the window, but I gave the bottle a good shaking, and made the frogs keep quiet.

Many attempts have been made to describe the sounds made by frogs. That of the African *Kassina senegalensis*, for example, has been said to resemble a cork being drawn from a bottle. In 1975 the Audubon Society in the United States published a report to enable urban visitors to identify frogs by their sounds:

American toad:	trilling
Fowler's toad:	nasal bleat
Green frog:	like a plucked banjo string
Grey tree frog:	short, harsh trill
Leopard and pickerel frogs:	resembles snoring
Spring peeper:	like sleigh bells
Wood frog:	creaky clatter

More specific lists have been compiled to describe the range of sounds made by the largest of the American frogs, the bullfrog, *Rana catesbeiana*. Suggestions range across:

jug-o'-rum
more rum
blood 'n' ouns
br-wum
be drowned
knee deep
bottle-o'-rum

According to natural history artist Mark Catesby in his *The Natural History of Carolina* (1731-43), 'The noise they make has caused their name; for at a few yards distance their bellowing sounds very much like that of a bull a quarter of a mile off, and what adds to the force of the sound, is their sitting within the hollow mouth of the spring.'

Other frogs have also derived their names from their sounds: the Carpenter frog, *Rana virgatipes*, is so-called because it sounds like a carpenter hammering nails. The Barking frog, *Eleutherodactylus latrans*, found in the southern United States and northern Mexico, is said to sound like a fox-terrier, the Pig frog,

Rana grylio, like grunting pigs, and the Sheep frog, *Hypopachus cuneus*, from Mexico and Texas, resembles bleating sheep.

SOME FROG RECORDS

OLDEST INHABITANT
The Stephens Island Frog has been around for 170-275 million years, and is thought to be the ancestor of all frogs. Discovered in 1917, it is found only in New Zealand.

LONGEVITY
Toads appear to live longer than frogs, whose lifespan averages five or six years. In *The British Zoology* (1776), Thomas Pennant reported the authenticated story of a toad

Poised for a good croak — a South African bullfrog, Pyxicephalus adsperus.

The senior citizen of the frog world: a Stephens Island frog, Leiopelma hamiltoni.

that had lived with a British family for at least forty years — apparently the same one about which Gilbert White had written in 1768; it was ultimately attacked by one of their other pets, a raven, and died soon afterwards.

LARGEST

Although there are occasional unverified reports of frog monsters in the New Guinea forests, the world's largest known frog is the Goliath frog, *Rana goliath*, found in Zaire, Cameroun and Equatorial Guinea. In 1965, in the River Muni, the Spanish naturalist, Dr. Jorge Sabater Pi, caught a female that weighed 7lb 4¾oz with a toe-to-toe limb-span of 32¹⁄₁₀ inches (they have long legs though — their body, from 'snout to vent,' is closer to a foot long). A bullfrog weighing a similar amount and allegedly a yard long was found in Martha Lake, Washington, in 1949.

In the 1880s there was a giant frog living in Killarney Lake, New Brunswick, Canada, that was befriended by a local hotelier, Fred Coleman, and his customers, who fed it titbits until it grew to a huge size. Unfortunately, in 1885, two fishermen decided to enhance their catch by dynamiting fish from the lake, and killed the 'Coleman Frog' in the process. It was claimed that his body weighed in at an astonishing 42lb, and to this day his stuffed body can be seen in the York-Sunbury Historical Society Museum, Fredericton.

The largest British frog is the Marsh frog, *Rana ridibunda*, which can measure over five inches long and weigh as much as 11oz. These are not an indigenous species, but twelve adults were introduced from Hungary in 1935 into the Romney marshes, Kent, since when their croaking has been a source of annoyance to local inhabitants. *Rana temporaria*, the common frog, a British native, seldom exceeds 3¾ inches.

The largest British amphibian is the Common toad, *Bufo bufo*, measuring up to four inches long and weighing over a quarter of a pound.

The largest tree frog is *Hyla vasta*, which is found only on Hispaniola, at over five inches long, with huge round finger and toe disks which grip like superglue.

The world's largest toad is the South American Marine toad, *Bufo marinus* — specimens with a body length of over 9 inches and weighing almost 3lbs have been recorded. Though it is officially a resident of South America, it has become the most geographically dispersed amphibian, having been introduced everywhere in the world that sugar is grown in order to combat the ravages of sugar beetles — although they are unfortunately also responsible for killing off other local amphibians. In Australia, the Marine toad 'front' is moving south from Queensland, allegedly by their stowing away on trucks. Australian youths have devised a fiendish variation on golf, using them as balls.

SMALLEST

The world's smallest toad is the East African toad, *Bufo taitanus beiranus*, from Mozambique. Full-grown adults seldom attain one inch long.

The world's smallest tree frog is appropriately called the Least tree frog, *Hyla ocularis*, found in the southeast United States; its maximum length rarely exceeds $^{11}/_{16}$ inch.

The world's smallest amphibian is the Cuban arrow-poison frog, *Sminthillus limbatus*, a bare $^1/_3$–$^1/_2$ inch long. The South African Chitiala frog, *Phrynobatrachus natalensis*, is around half an inch long.

BEST AND WORST JUMPERS

Because their metabolism is very slow, frogs are capable of jumping only in short bursts before resting, exhausted. A Spring peeper, *Hyla crucifer*, has been recorded as making 120 consecutive (and progressively shorter) jumps, but this is exceptional.

A Sharp-nosed frog, *Rana oxyrhyncha*, known as 'Leaping Lena' (though actually a male), measuring less than two inches long, was entered for a leaping contest at a Frog Olympics in Cape Town on 18 January 1954, competing against much larger Long-toed or Dusky-throated frogs (*Rana fuscigula*) which were typically executing triple jumps of about 9 feet. Dr Walter Rose, a scientist who had been studying frog leaps, observed the contest and reported on Lena's performance:

Seeing the tiny chap squatting there, the crowd began to laugh, then as he stayed blinking in the unaccustomed light, they commenced to jeer. Our hearts alternated between our mouth and our boots, for we were in effect his sponsor. Then, to our joy, the little fellow braced himself together, inflated his little chest, and leapt; once, twice, three times in a straight line. At the first leap the crowd gasped; at the second it cried out in amazement and at the third tumult broke out.

Lena had covered 24 feet 3½ inches — and later broke his own record with a triple-jump of 32 feet 3 inches. He had thus leaped almost 200 times his own length, equivalent to a human triple-jump of over a quarter of a mile!

On 21 May 1977, another Sharp-nosed frog — a female called 'Santjie' — leaped 33 feet 5½ inches in three consecutive leaps at a frog derby at Larula Natal Spa, Paulpietersburg, South Africa.

American bullfrogs are such enthusiastic jumpers that they have to be restrained.

The longest single frog jump on record is one of 20 feet 3 inches, by a frog named 'Davey Croakett,' owned by Dennis Matasci, at an Angel's Camp, California, jumping contest in 1976 (see also page 62).

The tiny Greenhouse frog, *Eleutherodactylus ricordi planirostris*, is perhaps the worst jumper, capable of less than 5 inches.

The Cricket frog, *Acris crepitans*, less than 1⅜ inches long, can jump thirty-six times its own length: if a six foot man jumped thirty-six

A small but deadly arrow poison frog.

times his own length, the long-jump record would stand at 216 feet!

MOST DANGEROUS
The *Dendrobatidae*, or 'arrow-poison' frogs of Central and South America, are the most deadly. Despite its diminutive size, the world's most poisonous amphibian is the Golden dart-poison frog, *Phyllobates terribilis*, of Western Colombia. The skin secretions of one adult contain 1,100 micrograms of a toxic poison — sufficient to kill 2,200 people.

FASTEST FROGS
In leaping contests, speeds of up to 18mph have been recorded.

MOST PROLIFIC
The Marine toad, *Bufo marinus*, lays 35,000 eggs a year.

LEAST PROLIFIC
The Cuban arrow-poison frog, *Sminthillus limbatus*, lays only one egg a year.

COMMONEST
The Marine toad, *Bufo marinus*, is actually commoner than the so-called Common toad.

MOST WIDE-RANGING HABITAT
The Green toad, *Bufo viridis*, has been found 26,246 feet up the Himalayas and toads have been found more than 1,000 feet down a coalmine.

RAREST
The world's rarest amphibian is the Israel painted frog, *Discoglossus nigriventer* — only five have been recorded since 1940.

FASTEST DEVELOPMENT
Tadpoles of *Atelopus stelzneri*, a black toad found in Uruguay, emerge a day after the eggs are laid.

FROGS AND MAN

USEFUL FROGS
FROG RAISING FOR PLEASURE AND PROFIT

Dr Albert Broel was perhaps the greatest frog farmer of the twentieth century. Describing himself as the 'Originator of Canned Frog Legs,' he left a substantial record of his life with frogs in an extraordinary book, *Frog Raising for Pleasure and Profit*, which went through several expanded editions between 1937 and 1950. With evident justification, he claims that his firm, The American Frog Canning Company, based in New Orleans, was 'the largest breeders, packers and shippers of frogs in the world'. He embarks on a history of frog farming, noting such incidental information as that in 1938 Germany was experimenting with high-fashion frogskin shoes and that at great expense Mussolini had imported frogs by air from the United States to Italy. In the often bizarre chapters that follow, he gives the full low-down on the commercial aspects of 'frog culture' — especially that of American Giant Bullfrogs. He advises on 'getting acquainted with frogs',

Dr Broel's letterhead, listing some of his extensive range of frog products.

Inset: Dr Broel comments: 'Even children can handle giant bullfrogs'.

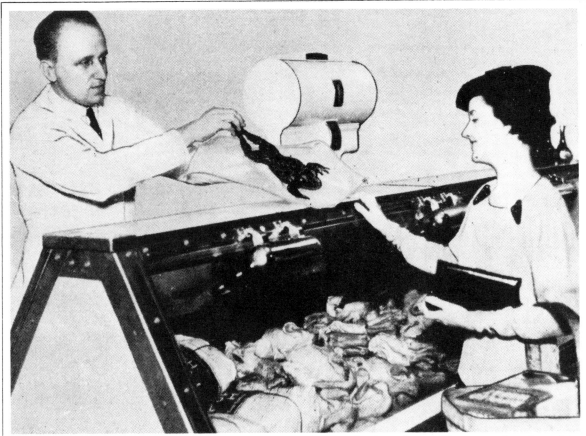

'Will there by anything else, Madam?' An illustration of the profit side of Frog Raising for Pleasure and Profit.

recommending that a would-be frog breeder might raise 5,000 to 10,000 frogs per acre, and offers detailed instructions on building special ponds, breeding and feeding frogs and marketing them. Photographs show his streamlined slaughter houses and canning plants, and ladies calmly receiving enormous frogs over the counter at a butcher's. Dr Broel himself clearly made a fortune from his enterprise: pictures depict his huge factories — one of them flanked with giant statues of frogs with electric lights for eyes. In his brief autobiography he notes his lifelong interest in frog farming: 'As far back as I can remember, my mother used to say, "Son, if you want to make a success in life — Raise Frogs".'

Dr Broel's pioneering work continues today. A typical American frog farm of the 1980s is that of John Aderhold of Long Branch, Texas. Called, the Goggle Eye Frog Farm, it is a forty-acre farm of ponds and woodland, with a tin 'frog-house' where the tadpoles are placed to develop. Established in 1969, within three years it was supplying over 10,000 frogs per annum, principally to educational and scientific research institutions — though this is a drop in the frog pond compared with the fifteen million per annum that are used in the United States. Interestingly, Mr Aderhold was formerly in the navy — as a frogman! Among other frog farms are the Southern Frog Company, Dumas, Arkansas and El Froggo Estates in Illinois. In Taiwan, an enterprising frog farmer called Cheng Chiun breeds giant bullfrogs imported from the United States, feeding them on potato crisps when small, and ground fish and snails later. Within thirteen years of establishing his business, it was reported, he had 40,000 frogs.

TOADS IN THE GARDEN

'The toad, without which no garden would be complete.'
[CHARLES DUDLEY WARNER, *MY SUMMER IN A GARDEN*, 1870]

He is not John, the gardener,
And yet the whole day long
Employs himself most usefully,
The Flower beds along.

He is not Tom, the pussy-cat,
And yet the other day,
With stealthy stride and glistening eye,
He crept upon his prey.

He is not Dash, the dear old dog,
And yet, perhaps, if you
Took pains with him and petted him,
You'd come to love him too.

He's not a Blackbird, though he chirps,
And though he once was black;
And now he wears a loose grey coat,
All wrinkled on the back.

He's got a very dirty face,
And very shining eyes!
He sometimes comes and sits indoors;
He looks — and p'r'aps is — wise.

But in a sunny flower-bed
He has his fixed abode;
He eats the things that eat my plants —
He is a friendly Toad.

[JULIANA HORATIA EWING, *A FRIEND IN THE GARDEN*]

Roman writers Apuleius and Pliny both recommended burying a toad in a pot to prevent storm damage to fields. This strange horticultural tip persisted well into Elizabethan times: Thomas Hyll, author of a gardening treatise published in 1593, suggested dragging a toad around the garden before sowing seeds. The animal was then to be placed in an earthenware pot and buried in a flower bed, to 'prevent creeping things'. Before the plants grew, though, it had to be exhumed, or the vegetables would taste bitter.

Such fantasy aside, in fact toads are genuinely useful in any garden because they eat insects which damage plants. The American herpetologist, Mary Cynthia Dickerson, writing early this century, even went so far as to calculate the precise monetary value of a toad in the garden. She estimated that 88 per cent of a toad's diet consists of insects that are regarded as harmful garden pests. In three months, she estimated, a toad would consume 9,936 injurious insects, of which 1,988 (16 per cent) were cutworms (moth caterpillars). Based on cutworm damage alone, and reckoning this damage as valued at a conservative one cent per cutworm per annum, Miss Dickerson showed that a toad in the garden could thus save at least $19.88 per annum — and that was at 1906 prices. She reported an actual case of the writer, Celia Thaxter, author of *Island Garden*, who had imported sixty toads into her garden to conquer a plague of slugs. As summer passed, the toads '... grew fatter and fatter till they were round as apples,' and her plants were unmolested by any slug or insect pests.

Fine weather forecast: a frog barometer predicts improving conditions.

THE FROG BAROMETER
'For they were yellow in the sun and brown in rain.'
[SEAMUS HEANEY, *THE DEATH OF A NATURALIST*, 1966]

Frogs have long been believed to have the power of weather forecasting, and so frogs have been widely used as barometers. In Germany, tree frogs were once kept in glass jars equipped with tiny ladders; in fine weather they climbed the ladders, but stayed snugly at rest in poor weather.

FROGBAIT
Put your hook through your frog's mouth, and out at his gills, and then with a fine needle and silk sew the upper part of his leg with only one stitch to the arming wire of your hook, or tie the frog's leg above the upper joint to the armed wire; and in so doing use him as though you loved him, that is, harm him as little as you may possibly, that he may live the longer.
[IZAAK WALTON, *THE COMPLEAT ANGLER I*, 1653]

THE SCIENTIFIC FROG
'Given its anatomy, the frog, more than any of the cold-blooded animals, anticipates man.'
[CARL JUNG]

The frog has been of inestimable importance in major scientific experiments. The Dutch natural history pioneer, Jan Swammerdam (1637-85) once commented, 'I would on first setting out inform the reader that there is a

Izaak Walton, master angler — and somewhat perverse frog-lover.

much greater number of miracles and natural secrets in the frog than anyone hath ever before thought of or discovered.' His study of frog reproduction was the standard authority on the subject for many years. William Harvey (1578-1657), whose *De Motu Cordis* (1628) first explained the circulation of the blood, based much of his research on the frog. Within a few years of Harvey's death, Marcello Malpighi (1628-94), an Italian biologist, by studying the lungs of frogs, discovered the minute capillary blood vessels that connect the veins to the arteries — the final component in our understanding of blood circulation. The microscopic studies of the frog's anatomy by Antonie van Leeuwenhoek (1632-1723) provided further important information about this subject. It was the accidental discovery of the effect of touching a frog's leg with two metals by Luigi Galvani

A replica of 2nd century AD Chinese astronomer Chang Heng's seismoscope, or earthquake detector: tremors caused delicately balanced balls to fall from the dragons' mouths into those of the frogs.

(1737-98) that led to further significant advances in the understanding of electricity: one day in his Bologna laboratory, a frog's leg lying on a zinc plate was touched with a steel scalpel and twitched. Galvani believed that he had discovered 'animal electricity,' and devoted the rest of his life to investigating the phenomenon. After Galvani's death, his countryman, Count Alessandro Volta (1745- 1827), showed the true cause of this reaction — and in so-doing invented the battery.

For two hundred years the frog has been found to be one of the most useful of laboratory animals, in research and in teaching

18th-century experimental apparatus demonstrating that electricity causes muscular contraction in frogs' legs.

fundamental aspects of anatomy and biology, such as reproduction, digestion and respiration. It even inspired the frogman's flipper: based on the design of the frog's foot, it was invented in 1927 by Louis de Corlieu of France. *Xenopus* (the African clawed toad) was formerly used in pregnancy testing — and nearly became extinct before the technique was replaced by chemical methods. The ability of frogs to regenerate certain parts of their bodies, and to accept transplanted organs, has been a vital component of research into recent human organ transplant. There are even plans to put frogs into space: George W. Nace of the University of Michigan's Amphibian Faculty has proposed putting frogs into orbit via a space shuttle to test the effect of weightlessness on breeding: another Giant Leap for Mankind — with a little help from the frog.

FROGS AT PLAY

The attributes of frogs have been widely emulated by man in a variety of games. Leapfrog has been played since Medieval times or earlier — Jan Breughel depicted it in several paintings. There was also a Medieval game known as *La Grenouille*, 'The Frog,' though the rules of it have been lost. 'The Frog Dance,' in which people squatted down and kicked their legs like frogs, was also once popular. 'Frog-in-the-middle' (a northern England version of 'Pig-in-the-middle') was a game in which four or more people, with one of them in the middle, buffeted the 'frog' until he caught one of them, who took his place. It is described in Thomas Wright's *History of Domestic Manners* (1862). The rhyme, 'A gaping wide-mouthed waddling frog' appears to have started out as part of an eighteenth-century family game that

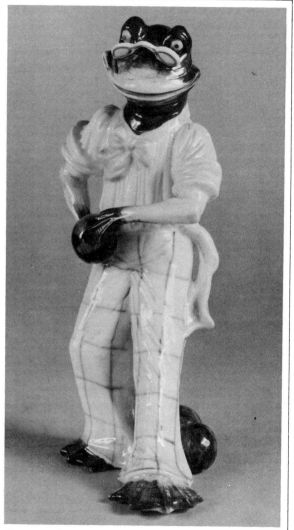

Frogs' legs before wicket — a pair of sporting cricket frogs.

Beer and skittles in the frog world — a Victorian ceramic bowling frog.

involved questions and forfeits; it appeared in *Top Book* published in about 1760, and directions for playing it appeared in C. Shepard's *Mirth Without Mischief* of c.1780. 'Jiggle-Joggle' was a short-lived game that involved racing cardboard frogs along lengths of string.

Frog jumping contests, pioneered among gambling prospectors in the nineteenth-century gold rushes, are still held in the United States. In Sacramento, California, William Steed set up Croaker College to train frogs for such contests. Graduates of the College (tuition fees $50 per annum or more) include President Reagan's 'Jelly Bean' and Dolly Parton's 'Dolly Do' — who wore a pink bikini. Other celebrity owners have included folksingers Johnny Cash and Glen Campbell, and Dinah Shore. Mr Steed has a bumper sticker on his car reading 'Support Your Local Frog'.

FROGS IN THE NEWS

Not all frogs live placidly in the wild: every now and then man makes a celebrity out of the odd frog:

FROGS AND THE ROYALS

There is a legend that King John, who died on 19 October 1216, was poisoned by a toad; a monk at Swineshead Abbey, where the King stayed after losing his baggage train in the Wash and before moving to Newark (where he died), overheard John threatening to raise the price of bread:

> Then yede the Monke into a gardeyne, and fonde a grete tode therein, and toke her up and put her in a cuppe and pryked the tode through with a broche many times tyll that venym came out of evry syde in the cuppe. And he toke the cuppe and filled it with good ale, and brought it before the Kynge ... within two dayes hee deyed ...

[WILLIAM CAXTON, *CHRONICLE OF ST ALBANS*, 1502]

The Frog Race Game

JIGGLE-JOGGLE

The "SOCIETY PICTORIAL" says
"A good indoor game...very exciting .... splendid fun for both big and little people."

"TIT BITS" the well known weekly says
"There is nothing to approach 'Jiggle-Joggle':- indeed it promises to become quite a feature at festive gatherings."

BY ROYAL   LETTERS PATENT

For a jig with "Jiggle-Joggle"
And the wiggle-waggle-woggle
Of the frogs is not considered
infra dig.

"It's a game that will not bore you
And the youngsters they'll adore you
For that 'Jiggle-joggle-jiggle-joggle-jig'."

BRITISH MANUFACTURE.

Fun with frogs in the drawing room.

In 1875, Queen Victoria was not amused by a sudden invasion of frogs — appropriately at Frogmore House, near Windsor. Prince Christian of Schleswig-Holstein-Sonderburg, the Ranger of Windsor Great Park, wrote to the naturalist, Frank Buckland:

> There is a plague of frogs at Frogmore and the Queen wishes me to write to you as she is anxious that you should come down tomorrow, Friday, to ascertain what could be done to get rid of them. It seems that it is something quite extraordinary.

Buckland set ducks on them, which apparently did the trick.

FROGGIES

The French are called 'frogs' or 'froggies' not only because they eat them, but because the

The monk and toad that killed King John.

Buckland — Victoria's frog exterminator.

33

Nostradamus (1503-66) — in his predictions he called the French 'toads'.

coat of arms of Paris featured three frogs or toads — 'three toads erect, saltant,' according to Guillim's *Display of Heraldrie* (1610). The phrase, 'qu'en disent les grenouilles?' — 'what do the frogs (Parisians) say?' — was often used at the French court. 'Froggy' does not appear to have come into widespread use in English, however, until the 1870s.

In one of his predictions, Nostradamus called the French 'crapauds' (toads): 'Les anciens crapauds prendront Sara' — 'The old toads will take Sara'. 'Sara' is Aras backwards, and the prophecy was believed to have been fulfilled when Louis XIV took Aras from Spain.

French Aristocrats often made peasants spend the night beating the surface of ponds to quieten frogs in the breeding season; this became one of the many grievances that led to the French Revolution of 1789!

It is said that in about 1800, a creole, Bernard Marigny, introduced a dice game into New Orleans; he was nicknamed 'Crapaud' ('Johnny Crapaud' — the local equivalent of the English 'froggy' — was a slang term for a Frenchman), and the game thus became known as 'craps'.

In January 1954 there was a report of an invasion of French edible frogs, *Rana esculenta*, that had somehow crossed the English Channel and were eating the common frog, *Rana temporaria*, in southern England. The expeditionary force had apparently moved as far north as Hampstead Ponds, London.

FROG FREAKS

In October 1957, a twenty-legged frog was found in Amsterdam; rumours of mutation caused by radioactive waste were soon rife. In August 1968, the Japanese newspaper, *Asahi Shimbun*, reported the discovery of a frog with ten legs, prompting a similar outcry.

DESIGNER FROGS

In 1975, Associated Press reported the bizarre pastime of one Clarence McKosky, a mail clerk at the University of California at San Diego. Having failed to raise a frog-jumping champion, at various charity functions during the early 1970s he had been exhibiting frogs dressed in specially designed costumes, including a cavalier, a calypso dancer and a Playboy Bunny. He remarked, 'The most difficult part is fitting the pattern. You have to be careful not to stick them with pins.'

HELP A TOAD ACROSS THE ROAD

In April 1970, frog crossing signs were erected in Switzerland where frogs crossing roads to spawn had become a serious wet-weather hazard. In 1977 it was reported from Bavaria that frog underpasses were being built.

In Britain there has been widespread concern about declining numbers of ponds — in 1970 'Save the Frog' was launched by the Wildlife Youth Service of the World Wildlife Fund and in 1973 Operation Tadpole was launched to place frog spawn in 'safe' ponds. A much-publicised 'Help a Toad Across the Road' campaign was recently organised by the British Fauna and Flora Preservation Society. After somehow estimating that twenty tons of toads are squashed on British roads every year, they erected a number of toad crossings, devising a graphic roadsign to indicate them. In spring 1985, official toad crossing signs were introduced, and the 1985 winner of the Wildlife Photographer of the Year contest was Ian West, for his photograph of a toad crossing a road.

FROG CRASH HORROR

In 1981 the *Washington Post* reported that a woman in Maine bought a potted plant at Sampson's Supermarket, Damariscotta; as she drove home to Round Pond, she looked over her shoulder and saw a '... reptile-like creature darting its tongue at her'. Unnerved, she crashed her car — and promptly sued the supermarket for negligence in selling a plant containing what turned out to be a tiny tree frog.

CROAK AND DAGGER

In 1981 a frog battle was reported from the Chinese province of Hunan. Meng Tou, the major of Huitong, wrote:

There was a tremendous noise in the middle of the night. I made my way towards its source and there I saw more than 2,000 frogs engaged in a bloody conflict, watched by about 50,000 other frogs who were croaking away at the top of their voices. Some frogs were engaged in single combat. Others were mounting collective assaults. Then the frogs formed up into a column forty metres long and three metres wide and marched away, past the Shangweidian Commune Clinic, leaving their dead and wounded behind.

FROGS AND THE LAW

Although it is permitted to catch common species, the 1981 British Wildlife and Countryside Act makes it illegal to sell common frogs or toads or tadpoles without a licence from the Department of the Environment. The Natterjack toad in particular is a protected species, making it illegal to take them from the wild or to kill them. It is also illegal to import frogs into Britain, and to release alien species into the wild.

COSTLY NEW HOME FOR TOADS

In December 1985, British Nuclear Fuels announced that they planned to spend £1 million to create a breeding ground for a small colony of Natterjack toads which were unfortunately living in the path of a proposed railway track at their plant at Sellafield in Cumbria. As the colony comprised about 500 Natterjacks, their new habitat was estimated to be costing £2,000 per toad.

'TOE OF FROG':
FROGS IN MYTH AND MAGIC

FROGLORE — FROG BELIEFS AROUND THE WORLD

In innumerable folk beliefs in most parts of the world, the frog has been associated with the moon, with water and resurrection; it was a positive symbol of fertility, creation, evolution and wisdom — though occasionally it has also been regarded as possessing certain less appealing qualities, such as being 'unclean,' vain, lazy and cold. Since the toad was believed to be poisonous, its symbolism is characteristically more negative.

The Bible strangely fails to mention toads, but there is a Biblical abhorrence of frogs. *Exodus* 8 concerns the plague of frogs that befalls Egypt, and *Revelation* 16 contains a reference to '... three unclean spirits like frogs'.

EGYPT

The ancient Egyptian goddess Heket, wife of Khnum, has a frog's head. Heket and Khnum were the first to 'build men and make gods'. Heket sometimes appears as a frog, sometimes as a human with a frog's head. She is present at the birth of royal babies, and is represented on sarcophagi and in death scenes. A cult associated with Heket was practised at Abydos in the Nineteenth Dynasty (c1350–1200 BC) — a stone carving of the frog goddess has been found at the temple there, and another at Denderah shows a frog seated at the foot of Osiris. Horus, the sun god, was born out of a lotus, but in some versions of the legend was also born under the protection of a frog goddess, so the frog became closely associated with lotus and lily. Models of frogs appear in Egyptian tombs and on amulets and bracelets found on mummies from all periods. The Egyptian hieroglyph for an 'unfinished human' or

Egyptian Pharaoh Seti I makes an offering to the frog-goddess Heket at Abydos.

embryo, was a frog, and a frog was sometimes used as a symbol for a large number, or specifically 100,000. This, and its other associations, largely derived from the sudden and seemingly miraculous appearance of huge numbers of frogs at times of rainfall. Similar beliefs persisted elsewhere along the Nile: in his *Missionary Travels* (1857), David Livingstone wrote of the *matlamétlo*, a frog believed to appear with the rain, and hence from the clouds. He reported that the rising Nile and the appearance of frogs were thus connected, and closely associated with fertility beliefs. Frog amulets were therefore worn to ensure fertility — and even eaten by some African tribes to achieve this end. Elsewhere in Africa, the frog is one of the commonest animals in rain-making ceremonies. Bechuana warriors also wore frog skins to make

A Graeco-Roman oil lamp of 3rd-4th century AD — the frog is a symbol of resurrection.

them slippery in battle, and the powerful thighbones of the giant Goliath frog were believed to be lucky.

EUROPE

The belief, like that of ancient Egypt, that frogs are generated spontaneously from mud and sun, led to the association of frogs with fertility cults. Votive frogs were once sacrificed in the ancient Greek temple of Artemis Orthia, Sparta. The Greek playwright Aristophenes' frogs chorus and other theatrical frog mimes were associated with resurrection beliefs, and in the Roman writer Juvenal's *Satires*, the Stygian pool of the underworld contained frogs. Graeco-Roman and Coptic art often features symbols of frogs connected with resurrection. The Roman historian, Pliny, in his *Natural History*, recalled the Egyptian belief that frogs are dissolved in mud and spontaneously re-created: '. . . and strange to say, after six months of life they melt invisibly back into mud, and again in the waters of springtime are reborn what they were before.' Another Roman writer, Ovid (43 BC — AD 17), in his *Metamorphoses*, which describes all manner of wonderful transformations, presented a curious amalgam of folklore and scientific observation in his remark that 'Mud contains germs that produce green frogs; these have no legs when they are first born, but soon acquire limbs suitable for swimming and, to enable them to make long jumps on land as well, the hind legs are longer than the front.'

Philaster, a Medieval Bishop of Breschia, condemned frog-worshippers. The Italian custom of children using frog rattles at Easter, the *canta rana*, or 'frog sings', may relate to this little-known cult.

In many myths, the toad appears as the guardian of the Tree of Knowledge. The toad was also believed to attract poison, and they were thus put into wells to keep them pure. The Frankish kings' coat of arms once was three toads; this was converted to lilies, or fleur de lis, after the conversion of Clodvig to Christianity.

Frogs have been found as fertility amulets in the graves of Viking women, and in Sweden and Germany, at the time of childbirth, bread was once baked in the shape of frogs. A stone toad in the doorway of Friesing Cathedral is said to have been an offering in celebration of the birth of a son to Beatrix, wife of Emperor Frederick I, in 1164. Throughout the Middle Ages, complex frog symbolism persisted in art: in Hieronymus Bosch's painting, *The Seven Deadly Sins*, for example, 'Superbia', pride, is depicted as a naked woman with a frog on her pudendum.

There was a belief that the sex of unborn children can be predicted with frogs: one is dropped near a pregnant woman — if it falls on its belly, the child will be a boy, if on its back, a girl. Many other strange beliefs about frogs were also prevalent: they were once carried round cornfields and, before sowing, buried in the centre, then dug up before harvest. The toad featured widely in many

'Pride' with a frog in Hieronymus Bosch's The Seven Deadly Sins *(1475-80).*

supernatural happenings and prodigies: Ulisse Aldrovandi (1522-1605) reported that in Thuringia in 1553 a woman gave birth to a toad.

TOADSTONES

There is found in the heades of old and great toades a stone, which they call borax, or stolon: it is most commonly found in the head of a hee toade, of power to repulse poisons, and that it is a sovereraigne medicine for the stone [gallstones, etc].

[PIERRE BOAISTUAU *CERTAINE SECRETE WONDERS OF NATURE, 1569*]

39

Sleep my child:
The dark dock leaf
Spreads a tent
To hide your grief.
The thing you saw
In the forest pool
When you bent to drink
In the evening cool
Was a mask that He,
The Wisest Toad,
Gave us to hide
Our precious load —
The jewel that shines
In the flat toad-head
With gracious sapphire
And changing red.
For if, my toadling,
Your face were fair
As the precious jewel
That glimmers there,
Man, the jealous,
Man, the cruel,
Would look at you
And suspect the jewel.
So dry the tears
From your horned eyes,
And eat your supper
Of dew and flies;
Curl in the shade
Of the nettles deep.
Think of your jewel
And go to sleep.

[STELLA GIBBONS, 'LULLABY FOR A BABY TOAD']

A widespread belief is that the toad has a precious stone or jewel in its head — symbolizing the idea that virtue can be concealed beneath an ugly appearance. Thomas Lupton, in his *One Thousand Notable Things* (1579), explains that, 'A toad-stone (*crapaudina*) touching any part envenomed, hurt, or stung with rat, spider, wasp, or any other venomous beast, ceaseth the pain or swelling

Removing a priceless toadstone — from Hortus Sanitatis *(1490).*

thereof.' Supposed lucky toadstones, sometimes known as bezoars, were once used as amulets and set in rings. The Roman philosopher, Aelian (third century BC), declared that people were killed instantly on drinking wine poisoned with toad blood. However, this venom could be readily detected by holding a toadstone near it. If poison was present, the toadstone would 'sweat'. The authenticity of a toadstone could be tested by presenting it to a toad — if it was genuine, the toad would try to snatch it from you. Actual 'toadstones' were probably sharks' teeth or various mineral substances sold by charlatans.

There may be many that wore these stones in Ringes being verily persuaded that they keep them from all manner of grypings and pains of the belly.
[EDWARD TOPSELL, *THE HISTORIE OF FOURE-FOOTED BEASTES*, 1607]

'It fareth with finer wits as it doth with the pearl, which is affirmed to be in the head of the toad.'
[THOMAS NASH, *THE ANATOMIE OF ABSURDITIE*, 1589]

THE FROG TRUTH DRUG

Giambattista Della Porta (*Magiae naturalis*, 1558, translated as *Natural Magick*, 1658) recommends doubting husbands who wanted to know 'How to force a woman to babble in her sleep whatever we desire to know her secrets', to put the tongue of a frog (or a duck) over his wife's heart as they 'give tongue at night'; he could then ask questions and get guaranteed truthful answers.

RAINING CATS AND FROGS

'Raining cats and dogs' is somewhat far-fetched. How much more probable, though, considering their aquatic habitat, that it should rain *frogs?* And indeed, since ancient times, frogs from heaven have been frequently reported. The belief is certainly widespread: 300 years before Christ, Aristotle called frogs 'Messengers of Jupiter,' and in ancient China the belief that frog spawn falls from heaven with the dew led to frogs being known as 'Heavenly Children'. In the first century AD the Roman writer, Pliny, described rains of frogs, as did the early third century Greek chronicler, Athenaeus. The Italian scientist Jerome Cardan included them in his book, *De Subtilitae* (1549), and they featured in an account of remarkable phenomena, *Prodigiorum Ac Ostentorum Chronicon* (1557), by Conrad Lycosthenes.

In his *The Compleat Angler* (1653), Izaak Walton summarized these earlier writer's beliefs about downpours of frogs, quoting Pliny's notion that certain frogs:

. . . breed of the slime and dust of the earth, and that in winter they turn to slime again, and that the next summer that very slime returns to be a living creature . . . and Cardan undertakes to give a reason for the

A rain of frogs, from Conrad Lycosthenes' Prodigiorum Ac Ostentorum Chronicon *(1557).*

raining of frogs; but if it were in my power, it should rain none but water-frogs, for those I think are not venomous.

Not long afterwards, Giambattista Della Porta, still following these ideas, but with a note of scepticism, was writing in his *Natural Magick* (1658):

'Frogs are wonderfully generated of rotten dust and rain; for a summer shower lighting upon the putrefied sands of the shore, and dust of the highways, engenders frogs ... the generation of them is easy, and sudden, that some write it hath rained frogs, as if they were gendered in the air.'

Sir Thomas Browne (1605-82), a somewhat eccentric writer and scientist, was convinced that the sun is '... fruitful in the generation of Frogs, Toads and Serpents'.

Samuel Pepys, attending an Ascension Day banquet hosted by the Lord Mayor of London on 23 May 1661, wrote in his *Diary*:

'At table I had very good discourse with Mr. Ashmole, where he did assure me that frogs and many other insects do often fall from the sky ready formed.'

In his *The Natural History of Staffordshire* (1686), Robert Plot, Keeper of the Ashmolean Museum in Oxford, referred to '... the ingenious author of *Mercuris Centralis*' who had reported '... that there is one at this time living that walking through a low marsh ground in England a foggy morning, had his hat almost covered with little frogs that fell on it as he walked'. In fact, recent evidence suggests that Plot was exceedingly gullible and swallowed the story of raining frogs as it was related to him by one Walter Chetwynd of Ingestre; on another occasion, Chetwynd, a noted practical joker, fed Plot venison and convinced him it was 'potted otter'. Plot described how Chetwynd's gatehouse roof was covered with frogs after a downpour. He thought it '... very improbable that they should either crawl up the walls, or leap up the stairs,' and so was inclined to follow Cardan's theory that frogs arose spontaneously from a peculiar kind of dust that settled on rooftops and germinated in the rain and sun:

... the Spawn or Seed of Frogs may be either blowne from the tops of Mountains, or drawn up with the Vapours out of uliginous [damp] places, and be brought to perfection in the Clouds, and discharged thence in Showers.

Gilbert White, author of *The Natural History of Selborne* (1788-89), described frog rains as 'that foolish opinion' — but could not resist giving an account of such an occurrence in Fulham.
The London *Mirror* of 4 August 1838 contained an account of a man who:

... states that, as he was walking up Tower Street on Monday afternoon, 30 July, 1838, saw some dozens of young frogs hopping on the foot and carriage pavements, which he conjectures had been precipitated to the earth in a heavy shower that had fallen about an hour before, as they were scattered to a considerable distance. He describes the largest of the frogs as not exceeding half an inch in length, while some were extremely minute, but all exceedingly lively.

On 16 June 1882, two live frogs were reportedly found *inside* a hailstone '... by the foreman of the Novelty Iron Works' at Dubuque, Iowa.

Many nineteenth-century travellers returned with tales of frog rains from around the world. Philip Gosse, in his *A Naturalist's Sojurn in Jamaica* (1851), recalled his visit to Haiti, where he encountered a large family of frogs in Port au Prince that was claimed locally to have descended from a rain of tadpoles some years before. In his memoirs, *Under Crescent and Star* (1895), Lt. Col. Andrew Haggard, Commander of the 1st Battalion of the Egyptian Army, described his experience of rains of toads occurring after sudden desert downpours:

One strange thing, noticeable in even the most sandy and previously driest parts of the desert just after this rain, was that the ground was covered with toads of all sizes. But these toads disappeared again as quickly as they had come. I could not find

Expecting rain — or a few friends dropping in? A froggy tableau of 1851.

one four days after the downpour. They must, therefore, either have come down in the rain or else up out of the ground, whither, I presume, they again retired to wait for the next flood, to come out again for a few more days enjoyment of life and liberty.

On 21 May 1921, the London *Evening Standard* reported:

SHOWER OF FROGS
Thousands of small hoppers fall at Gibraltar.
During a recent thunderstorm at Gibraltar a shower of frogs fell on the North Front. Thousands of these small hopping creatures, unusual at the Rock, may be seen in the hedges (says Reuter), and have aroused much curiosity.

The following year the London *Daily News* (5 September 1922) contained an account of 'little toads' that were said to have been falling for two days on Chalon-sur-Saône in France. On 14 August 1948, frogs rained down on Towyn, Merionethshire, Wales, in such abundance that '... brooms and shovels could hardly keep them out of houses'. On 12 June 1954, there was a rain of frogs at a naval display in Sutton Park, Birmingham, and in June 1979, a whole crop ranging from frog spawn through tadpoles to frogs was reported as having fallen in the garden of Mrs Vida McWilliam of Bedford.

Through all such accounts — and there is an astonishing number of them — there has been much argument as to the mechanism by which frogs fall from the sky. Sir George Duncan Gibb, describing a frog shower in Montreal in 1841, felt that waterspouts were responsible: frogs were sucked into the air and deposited often many miles away. Georg

Running for cover — a May 1958 Fate *feature on a shower of frogs.*

Hartwig in his *The Aerial World* (1874) dismissed the whole idea of frog rain in view of the fact that falling frogs would be squashed on impact, so in any sudden manifestation the frogs must have come *up* from the earth. He was particularly scathing of the idea of frogs being born in mid-air, which some earlier writers had asserted.

The eccentric American journalist Charles Fort (1874-1932) devoted most of his life to seeking out strange phenomena and was particularly interested in instances of things — especially frogs — falling from what he suggested might be a sort of suspended 'Super-Sargasso Sea' in the atmosphere, 'just beyond the reach of gravity'. All sorts of living and inanimate objects were, he believed, hovering in this mysterious outer world, ready to drop to earth when weather conditions were favourable. However, even he was suspicious of reports of showers of large frogs, and in 1926 he wrote to a friend, 'There may have been showers of adult frogs, but in my records, of about 80 instances, all showering frogs were little ones.'

Another investigator was Dr Eugene Willis Gudger of the North American Museum of Natural History, who in the 1920s wrote articles on the subject, coming down in favour of the waterspout theory. Like Gudger, a report in *Science* (7 June 1946) put the phenomenon down to whirlwinds carrying frogs from the surface of ponds, though recent research suggests that the case for cyclonic action remains unproven.

Ultimately, if mundanely, it seems most probable that frogs habitually emerge from their terrestrial hiding-places — sometimes suddenly and in very large numbers — after heavy rain, making it appear that they fell with the rain. Special heavy-duty anti-frog umbrellas will not, it appears, be necessary!

FROGSPELLS

Toad, that under cold stone
Days and nights hast thirty-one
Swelter'd venom sleeping got,
Boil thou first i' the charmed pot.

[SHAKESPEARE, *MACBETH IV.i.*]

Shakespeare ensured that the very first ingredient of the witches' brew was toad — and added 'toe of frog' for good measure. Frogs and toads were an essential ingredient in many spells: frog bones were widely used in magic potions, and judicious quantities of supposedly poisonous toad blood — the

UNUSUAL WEATHER WE'RE HAVING...

BUS STOP

'filthy toads' envenom'd gore' as Horace described it in his *Satires* — was used in love philtres. Frogs and frog bones were also used by the Romans as aphrodisiacs, but the early medical writer, Alexander Benedictus, reckoned that dried frog had the opposite effect, and Pliny's *Natural History* gave instructions on the use of frogs in spells to make women turn away from their lovers. A magic potion of toad spittle and sow thistle was said to be used to make witches invisible.

The toad was frequently regarded as a witch's helper, or 'familiar'. At Chelmsford in Essex in 1566, Elisabeth Francis, who was tried as a witch (she was imprisoned, but later tried on further charges and hanged in 1579), confessed that her cat turned into a toad, hopped into her husband's shoe and lamed him. Even a report of a toad being seen in a house was often sufficient 'proof' of witchcraft, as occurred in Somerset in 1530. In 1649 one John Palmer confessed at St. Albans that he had turned himself into a toad in order to torment a victim. A female spirit 'like a black toad' called Pigin, that apparently caused a child to become ill, appears in Ursula Kempe's confession in *A True and Just Record* of the St. Osyth witch trials of 1582.

An ancient Bohemian belief was that on St. George's Day, young men should catch frogs and wrap them in white cloths. At sunset, they would be placed on an anthill. When the ants had devoured the frogs, two of the bones were removed — one of them hook-shaped, one like a tiny spade. The hook was placed surreptitiously on a would-be lover's dress — she could then not resist falling in love with the man. When he tired of her, all he had to do was to touch her with the spade bone and the spell would be broken.

In Derbyshire, girls impaled frogs with pins and buried them. As in voodoo spells, straying lovers would experience deep pain and would return to their girlfriends; the pins would be removed, and a marriage would soon ensue.

In Yorkshire, a frog stuck with pins was left in a box until it died and withered; a bone was removed and attached to a man with the following incantation:

I do not want to hurt this frog,
But my true lover's heart to turn
Wishing that he no rest may find,
Till he come to me and speak his mind.

One of the 4 witches of Windsor, tried and executed in 1759, feeding her toad and cat familiars.

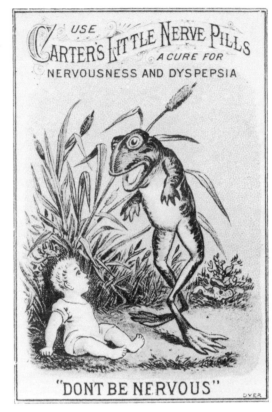

The cure-all frog relieves nervousness . . .

. . . and wards off pain.

FROGCURES

Experience has proved the toad to be endowed with valuable qualities. If you run a stick through three toads, and, after having dried them in the sun, apply them to any pest-

Toads dance at a gathering of witches.

ilent tumour, they draw out all the poison, and the malady will disappear.
[MARTIN LUTHER, *TABLE TALK*, 1569]

In days gone by, the frog was an indispensable item in the medicine cabinet. Pliny suggested rubbing arthritic limbs with live frogs — the theory was probably based on the agility of frogs and the suppleness of their legs. A more modern version of this, recorded in Utah, involved rubbing the joints with a roast frog. An inflamed eye could be cured by hanging the corresponding eye of a frog around one's neck. A frog's eye was also worn as a remedy for fever — but only if plucked out before sunrise. Marcellus, in his *De Medicamentis*, suggested catching a frog, spitting in its mouth and asking it to remove one's toothache; this technique was, however, regarded as unsuitable for women, since it would prevent them giving birth for a year. The Greek physician, Galen, offered a version of this involving boiling the frog in vinegar and using the resulting liquid as a mouthwash. Gargling with 'frog spit' was also widely recommended.

Hortus Sanitatis, a fifteenth-century medical encyclopaedia, contains instructions illustrated with woodcuts depicting the removal of toadstone and a lady using toads as treatment for 'apoplexy and choler' — apparently by putting one on her face! Epileptics were given powder made from frog's liver, while in Cheshire, unfortunate children who had thrush, a fungal disease of the mouth, could once have expected to be treated by having a live frog placed in their mouths; a Victorian woman who used the method was reported as remarking, 'I assure you we used to hear the poor frog whooping and coughing mortal bad for days after.' Similarly connecting the croak of the frog with that of such diseases as whooping cough, sufferers were once advised to place a frog in a box and suspend it round the patient's neck until the frog died — and with it the cough. Other froggy cure-alls included one for the removal of freckles, and frogs' ashes were believed to act as a depilatory — presumably because the frog itself is notably hairless. A seventeenth-century method of stopping bleeding was to bandage the wound with cloths dipped in '. . . ye green fome where frogges have their spawne three days before the new moon,' and an old Yorkshire remedy for constipation, cancer and other ailments and weaknesses was to swallow live baby frogs.

In parts of China, the Green tree frog, *Hyla annectens*, was known as the 'bamboo spirit,' since it was so elusive; if it was found among mulberries, it was especially prized for medicinal purposes, and was presented to the Emperor. Strangely, there may be some truth in one Chinese froggy cure: in ancient China, doctors included toad skin in various remedies for heart disease. Recent scientific analysis has shown that one of the chemicals present in the skin of certain toads resembles digitalis, which is used medically for the control of heart disorders.

TOAD EATING

'Be the most scorn'd Jack-Pudding of the
    pack,
And turn toad-eater to some foreign quack.'
[THOMAS BROWN (1663–1704), 'SATIRE ON AN IGNORANT QUACK', IN HIS *WORKS*, 1730]

'Toad-eating' was once a trick used by charlatans selling patent medicines: they would feed toads to an accomplice and then 'cure' them of the ill effects. Toad-eating or 'toady' thus came to mean any servile person, or sycophant.

FROG OMENS
In 1525, one John Mores of East Langdon, Kent, was said to be able to predict the future from the crawling of frogs — a technique known as theiromancy (divination by the observation of wild animals).

Frogs and toads have long been looked upon as portents:

LUCK
A frog brings bad luck if it enters a house.

If you see seven frogs at once, you will be rich.

Whatever you are doing when you hear the first frog, you will be doing for most of the year. (This belief comes from rural New England, and as what you were likely to be doing there was farming, and as farming was probably what you would be doing for the rest of the year, this could be the most accurate frog omen of all.)

It is unlucky to see a dead frog in the road — especially if you're a frog.

If the first frog you see in spring leaps into water, you will have bad luck; if it stays on the land, you'll shed as many tears as would be needed for the frog to swim away — you can't win!

WEATHER
When frogs in the grass appear bright yellowish-green, the weather will be fine; if dark and dirty, it will rain.

If the first frog you see is on the edge of a pool, it will be a dry summer.

Noisy frogs or a frog walking on a dry day are sure signs of rain.

If you kill a frog, it will rain for three days.

In America, after frogs are first heard in the spring, there will be three freezes until spring weather properly arrives; if not, a bad season follows.

Sap in maple trees will stop running when the frogs appear.

DEATH
If you see a frog in front of you and its mouth moves, it is counting your teeth — you must turn away or you will soon die.

A toad hopping over one's foot is a portent of death.

The Welsh say that if an Irishman spits on a frog, it will die.

THE IMMORTAL TOAD

I'd rather soar to death's abode
On eagle's wings, than 'live a toad'
Pent in a block of granite.

[JAMES SMITH (1775-1839), *CHIGWELL REVISITED*]

It has long been believed that toads can live sealed up in rocks. The idea stems partly, perhaps, from the fact that toads are cold and hence appear dead when they are alive. Robert Plot, the gullible seventeenth-century author who we met in the frog rain story, told of William Musgrove, Secretary of the Philosophical Society of Oxford, who had discovered a block of limestone:

> '... laid as a step-stone for passengers in the middle of a cartway between two rills [small streams] ... when a croaking noise being long time heard, and the parts near searched and nothing found, this stone at length was resolved should be broke, where in a cavity near the middle, a large toad was found, as big as a man's fist.'

On being released, the toad was alleged to have hopped about briskly. Plot went on to detail discoveries of living toads in flints found in German coalmines, inside tall oak trees and even, remarkably, in a stone removed from the steeple of Statfold that had been there for centuries. He speculated that toads might perhaps crawl into tiny cavities in rocks, and would then grow in them so they could not escape; how they got up steeples and tall trees he put down to the same mechanism that produced frog rainfall.

Plot's contemporary, John Evelyn, recorded in his *Diary* (23 July 1678) that he had been '... to see Mr Elias Ashmole's Library and Curiosities at Lambeth ... he shewed me a Toad included in Amber' — though there was no suggestion that if it were released it might hop about.

Dr William Buckland (1784-1856), Dean of Westminster and an eminent geologist, devised an experiment to test this belief. He built an apparatus consisting of twenty-four stone cells covered on one side with glass panels. Twelve of the cells measured 12×5 inches and were composed of coarse oolitic limestone; twelve were 6×5 inches and made of compact siliceous sandstone. In these chambers Buckland placed twelve large and twelve small toads, evenly distributed between limestone and sandstone, and on 26 November 1825 he covered the apparatus with three feet of earth. Within thirteen months, all the toads in the sandstone and the small toads in the limestone were dead. All the large toads in the limestone died within the next year. Apparently the toads in limestone had access to air and water, and possibly to food that permeated through the rock; the large ones were also able to consume their own body bulk and thus lived longer.

Robert Ripley, creator of the well-known 'Believe It or Not' newspaper column, reported:

> 'In the lobby of the new court house in Eastland, Texas, may be found the remains

'Scientific evidence' of a living entombed toad found in Sweden in 1733.

of 'Old Rip', a horned toad that lived without food or water for 31 years. Mr W.M. Wood of Eastland placed the toad in the corner-stone of the court house in 1897 and took it out alive on 17th February 1928. Old Rip was alive until January 1931, when he died of pneumonia.'

In fact, the whole story may well have been a practical joke perpetrated by Boyce House, editor of the Eastland daily paper; his publicity for it led to a national tour for Rip, including a meeting with President Coolidge at the White House. When Rip died, his body was exhibited in a satin-lined casket in Eastland County courthouse. Many people suspected House of having fabricated the tale, but when he died in 1961, he took the secret with him to the grave. And if it was truly a 'horned toad,' it doesn't really deserve a mention here anyway — horned toads are really lizards.

HATCHED BY A TOAD

The Basilsike ...
From powerful eyes close venim doth convey
Into the lookers hart, and killeth farre away.

[EDMUND SPENSER, *THE FAERIE QUEENE*, 1590]

The fabulous Basilisk or Cockatrice, 'King of the Serpents,' was regarded as the most deadly beast known: one glance caused certain death — though a weasel, a crowing cock or its own reflection could be used to combat it. It was said to hatch from an egg laid by a seven-year-old cock, when the dog star Sirius was in the ascendant — and to be hatched by a toad: the incubation period might be as much as nine years.

THERE ARE NO TOADS IN IRELAND

It has long been believed that there are no toads in Ireland because — along with the snakes — they were driven out by St. Patrick. In about 1188 Giraldus Cambrensis (c1147-1223), a Welsh historian, wrote *The Topography of Ireland*, an account of the country's history, geography, and natural history, in which he speculated that as a result of '... some hidden force of the land itself that is inimical to poisons, no poisonous animal can live here'. He also reported that:

'I have heard merchants that ply their trade on the seas say that sometimes, when they had unloaded their cargoes at an Irish port, they found toads brought in by chance in the bottom of the holds. They threw them out still living on to the land; but immediately they turned their bellies up, burst in the middle, and died, while everybody saw and wondered.'

Giraldus reckoned too that toads could not grow in Ireland because the mud did not contain the special 'seeds from which green frogs are born'. He explained, though, that the magical properties of other Irish animals could be put to good advantage: thongs made from Irish animal hides were said to be an excellent antidote to toad bites — they were to be cut into tiny pieces and drunk in water. He himself had seen a toad encircled by a thong and quite unable to pass it; it was able to escape only by burrowing under the ground. So remarkable was the sight of a toad in Ireland, Giraldus declared, that when Duvenaldus or Domhnall, the King of Ossory, heard of one being sighted, he was terrified and said '... that reptile brings very bad news to Ireland'. In fact, although there are no indigenous frogs or toads in Ireland, there is a small colony of Natterjack toads that have managed to survive in the south west — without exploding!

TOAD MYTHS

Touching a toad is popularly believed to cause warts. It does not, but as the skin of

Toads and toadstools — a woodcut by German artist, Fritz Lang, 1914.

many toads contains a protective irritant in its parotid gland, handling them can cause a rash — and any dog or cat that has tried to eat a toad once will never try a second time! It is said that German violinists once deliberately handled toads before playing, in the belief that their secretions prevent the hands from perspiring. There is a belief that toads have some connections with toadstools: in fact, the name comes from 'tod' meaning death and 'stuhl' a chair. They were once called 'tode-stoles'.

TOADPOWER

There was a Cambridgeshire belief, said to be prevalent until the 1930s, that a bone taken from a toad gives power over horses. The toad was stripped of its flesh by being pinned on an anthill, after which its bones were hurled into a stream. One bone would actually float *upstream* — making a screaming sound; this would be recovered and would make the so-called 'toadman' powerful over horses. Some versions suggest that the toadman had to visit a stable or graveyard on three consecutive nights to challenge the devil for possession of the magic bone. In Devonshire, toads were once burned alive to drive out evil, and in Herefordshire a toad's heart was worn by thieves so they could steal without being discovered.

THOUGHT FOR THE DAY

There is a legend that St Beno, passing a marsh, heard a frog that was disturbing his devotions, and bade it to be quiet; he then reflected on the fact that the frog, as one of God's creatures, had every right to make his sound, and so urged him to recommence his croaking.

THE MIDWIFE FROG

The Wends, an ancient Slav tribe, believed that the frog rather than the stork brought babies.

NOT A BOHEMIAN RHAPSODY

In Bohemia, toads were believed to contain souls, and it was thus forbidden to kill them on All Saints' Day. However, at other times, it was open season on frogs: in one folk custom that took place at Pilsen, a local person was elected 'King'. Accompanied by a judge, a crier and a 'Frog-flayer,' a grisly ritual was enacted that involved hanging frogs. A similar ceremony took place at Plas — except there the frogs were beheaded. Both were believed to be vestiges of pagan rain charms.

FROG TOWN

In s'Hertogenbosch, the capital of North Brabant in the Netherlands — and, incidentally, the birthplace of the medieval painter, Hieronymus Bosch — there is an ancient annual pre-Lent 'Frog Festival' at which a 'Frog Prince' is elected. The name of the town is temporarily changed to 'Oeteldonk,' or 'Place of Frogs,' and is decorated with frog pictures. There is even a frog in its coat of arms.

ASIA

A Central Asian creation myth involves a frog. Two deities, Otshirvani and Chagan-Shukuty, came to earth and saw a frog. Otshirvani sat on it while Chagan-Shukuty dived beneath the waters. He came up with a little earth, which he sprinkled on the frog, who sank — leaving just enough earth for the gods to float on; this patch of earth eventually grew and became the world's land mass when Shulmus, an evil demon, tried to fling the divine pair off it.

In Altai Tartar mythology, the frog discovered a mountain containing birch and stones, from which fire was first made — hence the frog was regarded as the bringer of fire.

In Chinese legend, a three-legged toad, *hsia ma*, swallows the moon and causes eclipses. Chinese bronze drums decorated with frogs were beaten to produce rain, and *Ch'ing-wa Shen*, frog spawn, was worshipped for financial success and good health.

In Japan a frog known as *kawazu* is a symbol of energy and perseverance, while the toad is known as *gama*, an evil goblin: a magical mist wafts from his mouth, causing humans to see visions and luring men, animals and insects to their destruction.

As in China, among the Shan and Karen tribes of Burma, the frog was believed to cause eclipses by swallowing the moon, and Burmese frog amulets protected children from the evil eye.

The Newars of Nepal worship the frog in association with the demigod, Nagas, who causes rainfall — hence frogs are never wilfully injured.

There is a Bengalese legend of a golden frog of destiny, and in Central India, a frog is tied to a rod and carried from house to house by villagers singing:

'Send soon, O frog, the jewel of the water!
And ripen the wheat and millet in the field.'

In the Kumaon district of north-west India, during droughts a frog is fixed to bamboo or a tree with its mouth up in the belief that the god of rain will take pity on it and send rain. In the Muzaffarpur district of India, the cry of a frog is believed to be heard by the god of rain, so unfortunate frogs are crushed to death in order that their dying croaks bring rain. Certain other Indian frog rainmaking ceremonies are less cruel, and simply involve pouring water over frogs.

In Sri Lankan mythology, a frog supports the world beneath a turtle, a snake and a giant.

In Malaya, a brilliantly coloured frog, *Rhacophorus dennysi*, is highly revered, and during certain festivals is carried in a procession in a tiny chair.

The connection between frogs and fertility is exemplified in this 13th-14th-century gold disc from Ecuador, which combines a tree frog and a woman.

AUSTRALIA

In southeast Australia, aborigines feared to injure *Tidelek*, the frog, or *Bluk*, the bullfrog. They were said to be full of water, and in this area of often heavy rainfall, it was believed that floods would follow. The frog family was known as 'Bunjil Willung,' or Mr Rain. A folk tale concerns a frog that drank all the water, which had to be released by making him laugh.

NORTH AMERICA

Among the Plains Indians, the toad was the wife of the sun. The Thompson River Indians of British Columbia believed that killing a frog causes rain. Cherokee ball-players avoided eating frogs in the belief that they might acquire the brittle bones of the frog. A Huron Indian legend explained that all the water in the world was inside a giant frog; Ioskeha, the creation hero, stabbed it and thereby released the water for man's use.

The Southern toad, *Bufo terrestris*, found in the deep south of the United States, was believed to have the power to turn a person's eyes green.

CENTRAL AND SOUTH AMERICA

Pre-Columbian frogs made of gold were used to encourage rain. In ancient Mexico, fried or dried frog was used in fertility sacrifices to the maize god. The Aztecs of Mexico even had a magnificent frog goddess's temple.

In Argentina, there is a belief that if an aggressive and sharp-fanged (but non-

A Nasca pot featuring tadpoles and frogs.

poisonous) Horned frog or Bell's ceratophrys, *Ceratophrys ornata*, bites a horse, the horse will die.

In Venezuela, frogs were regarded as the 'Lords of the Waters' and were responsible for bringing rain — but if they failed in their duty, they were not too elevated to be soundly whipped.

'THE FROG PRINCE' AND OTHER FROGGY TALES

Frogs have appeared in literature since ancient times. Theocritus (c310-250 BC) wrote in his *Idylls*:

> The frog's life is most jolly, my lads; he has no care
> Who shall fill up his cup; for he has drink enough to spare.

An anonymous Greek poet wrote the Homeric-style *Batrachomyomachia*, or *Battle of the Frogs and Mice*, which satirises Homer's *Iliad*. In it, a mouse, Pricharpax, is kidnapped by the frog king, Physignathos.

A woodcut showing the Battle of the Frogs and Mice, with an audience of gods.

Crossing a river with the mouse on his back, the frog king is alarmed by a snake, dives under the water and the mouse is drowned. As a result the mice declare war on the frogs. The gods are involved, though Athena remains neutral because the mice have devoured her robes and the frogs keep her awake with their incessant croaking, and so she has no time for either side. Instead of the Trojan war that lasted ten years, the frogs and mice slug it out for just one day. Zeus starts out on the side of the mice, but later becomes partisan and sends crab reinforcements to aid the frogs, who consequently win.

Several of Aesop's *Fables* concern frogs. One tells of a frog and a mouse who fight over ownership of a marsh, but while they battle, a kite swoops down and carries them both off. In another fable, the frogs ask for a king, and Zeus throws a log into their pond. Rejecting 'King Log' they ask for a real king; irritated by their demands, Zeus sends a stork that eats them.

In Ovid's *Metamorphoses*, Leto [Latona in the Roman version], the mother of the twins, Apollo [Phoebus] and Artemis [Diana], was drinking from a lake in Lycia; local peasants gathering reeds tried to stop her and insulted her; she therefore changed them into frogs so

that they would spend eternity leaping in and out of their lake.

The frog often appeared in Classical literature as a maligned animal in order to make some moral point. Plutarch, for example, wrote, 'Though boys throw stones at frogs in sport, the frogs do not die in sport, but in earnest.' A version of this, 'Though this be play to you, 'tis death to us' [Sir Roger L'Estrange, English journalist (1616-1704)], became virtually a proverbial expression.

Shakespeare made frequent reference to frogs and toads: he called Richard III 'that foul bunch-back'd toad', and Othello declares,

Not quite the king they expected — Griset's illustration to Aesop's Fables.

The legend of Leto and the frogs on a 16th-century plate by Alfonzo Patanazzi.

'... I had rather be a toad,
And live upon the vapour of a dungeon,
Than keep a corner in the thing I love
For others' uses.'

John Milton, in *Paradise Lost*, has the devil squat beside Eve, not as a serpent, but in the form of a toad.

In a Bible of 1778, a translation of Psalm 105, verse 30, was supposed to read 'Their land brought forth frogs, yea, even in their king's chambers'. An unfortunate printing error converted 'even' into 'seven' — and this edition was henceforth known as the *Frog Prayerbook*.

In his *Sprüche in Prosa*, Johann Goethe made the profoundly philosophical observation that, 'There are not frogs wherever there is water, but wherever there are frogs, water will be found.' Mrs Leo Hunter, in Charles Dickens' *The Pickwick Papers* (1837), asks a more down-to-earth question:

A plague of frogs in the king's chambers.

Mark Twain's Jumping Frog *lecture poster*.

Can I unmoved see thee dying
On a log, expiring frog?

Mark Twain's *The Celebrated Jumping Frog of Calaveras County*, originally published in the New York *Saturday Press* (18 November 1865), related the tale of one Jim Smiley, the inveterate gambler of Angel's Camp, a Californian Gold Rush town, who in 1849 or 1850 trained his frog, 'Dan'l Webster', as an apparently unbeatable champion jumper. One day a stranger appeared and Jim bet him $40 that Dan'l Webster could outjump any frog. The stranger took the bet, but as he had not got a frog about his person with which to challenge Dan'l, Jim went off in search of one. While he was gone, the stranger spoon-fed the unfortunate Dan'l with lead shot, so that when Jim returned and the contest started, the 'Celebrated Jumping Frog' sat 'planted as solid as an anvil'. Jim lost his $40, but by the time he discovered the deception, the stranger was long gone. On 19 May 1928, to commemorate Mark Twain's popular story, frog jumping contests were held at Angel's Camp, and continue today.

In modern novels, John Steinbeck's *Cannery Row* (1945) contains a vivid description of an American frog hunt in which 600-700 bullfrogs are caught by a gang of men. In 1980, whilst the story was being filmed at MGM Studios, Culver City, 5,000 frogs that had been rented at $2 each, escaped and overran the set.

CHILDREN'S LITERATURE

The *Fables* of the French poet, Jean de La Fontaine (1621-95), contain a number of stories involving frogs. In the fairy stories of Charles Perrault (1628-1703), *Les Fées* (The Fairies), first published in 1697 (and in English in 1729), is often known as *Diamonds and Toads*. In it, a good girl who is kind to a fairy is rewarded by receiving the power, whenever she speaks, of flowers and precious stones issuing from her mouth; her unpleasant sister, who is rude to the fairy, is cursed with releasing from her mouth a flood of squirming snakes and toads.

The Frog Prince is an old tale that was first published by the Brothers Grimm. There are many versions of it, but essentially it concerns a princess who releases from his enchanted state a prince who has been turned into a frog by an evil witch.

In Robert Chambers' *Popular Rhymes of Scotland* (1842), 'The Well of the World's

End,' a supposedly old story, relates how a frog helps a girl who has been forced to collect water from a well in a sieve; she takes him home and he makes her chop off his head with an axe, whereupon he turns into a human.

Lewis Carroll's *Alice in Wonderland* (1865) features a Frog Footman, and in *Through the Looking Glass* (1872) Alice meets a frog with a cockney accent. 'The Frogs' Birthday Treat' appears in Carroll's *Sylvie and Bruno* (1889), in which frogs are taken to the theatre for a performance of various 'Bits of Shakespeare'. In the sequel, *Sylvie and Bruno Concluded* (1893), a pig bewails the fact that he cannot jump, but then:

> There was a Frog that wandered by —
> A sleek and shining lump:
> Inspected him with fishy eye,
> And said 'O Pig, what makes you cry?'
> And bitter was that Pig's reply,
> 'Because I cannot jump!'

The Frog Footman in Alice in Wonderland.

Alice meets the cockney frog gardener.

That Frog he grinned a grin of glee,
And hit his chest a thump.
'O Pig,' he said, 'be ruled by me,
And you shall see what you shall see.
This minute, for a trifling fee,
I'll teach you how to jump!'

Unfortunately, the pig jumps headlong at a pump and expires:

That Frog made no remark, for he
Was dismal as a dump:
He knew his consequence must be
That he would never get his fee —
And still he sits, in miserie,
Upon that ruined Pump!

'Toad of Toad's Castle' appears in a number of books of the 1950s and '60s by Alison Uttley (1884-1976). He is a story-teller extraordinaire, who on his visits to the Rose and Crown Inn enthralls Snug and Serena, the two children of the mouse landlord and his wife, William and Marie Field-Mouse.

The American author and illustrator, Arnold Lobel (b1933), has produced several books for small children featuring a jolly out-going Frog and a sad, selfish Toad. These include *Frog and Toad are Friends* (1970) and *Frog and Toad Together* (1972).

FROG POEMS

Of all the funny things that live
In woodland, marsh or bog.
That creep the ground or fly the air,
The funniest thing's the frog.

[ANON]

As other references throughout this book show, frogs and toads have been a some-times surprisingly popular subject of many hundreds of poems. Some attempt to point to the assumed character of certain members of the tribe: Don Marquis' poem, *warty bliggens the toad* concerns a toad who considers him-self the centre of the universe: the earth exists for the sole purpose of growing toadstools for him to sit under. Others are written by frog-lovers, such as Seamus Heaney, who, in his *The Death of a Naturalist*, refers to '... the warm thick slobber of frogspawn,' and describes how as a child he used to gather it in jamjars. Some poems about frogs are too sad to be repeated here: Christina Rossetti — clearly a frogophile, as her 'The Frog and the Toad' indicates — also wrote 'A Frog's Fate,' which describes a frog being run over by a

Arnold Lobel's endearing Frog and Toad.

waggon, and Richard Wilbur's 'The Death of a Toad' presents the sorry tale of toad who gets mangled in the blades of a lawn mower!

Hopping frog, hop here and be seen,
I'll not pelt you with stick or stone:
Your cap is laced and your coat is green;
Good-bye, we'll let each other alone.

Plodding toad, plod here and be looked at,
You the finger of scorn is crooked at:
But though you're lumpish, you're
   harmless too;
You won't hurt me, and I won't hurt you.

[CHRISTINA ROSSETTI, 'THE FROG AND THE TOAD']

I'm a Nobody! who are you?
Are you — Nobody — too?
Then there's a pair of us!
Don't tell! they'd advertise — you know!

How dreary — to be — somebody!
How public — like a Frog —
To tell one's name — the livelong June —
To an admiring Bog!

[EMILY DICKINSON (1830-86), FROM *THE LIFE AND LETTERS OF EMILY DICKINSON*, 1924]

The toad beneath the harrow knows
Exactly where each tooth point goes;
The butterfly upon the road
Preaches contentment to that toad.

[RUDYARD KIPLING, *PAGETT MP*]

Frogs sit more solid
than anything sits. In mid-leap they are parachutists falling
in a free fall. They die on roads
with arms folded across their chests and head high.
I love frogs that sit
like Buddha, that fall without parachutes, that die
like Italian tenors.
Above all, I love them because,
pursued in water, they never
panic so much that they fail
to make stylish triangles
with their ballet dancer's legs.

[NORMAN MACCAIG, *FROGS*]

NURSERY FROGS
He was a frog and she was frog,
And they built a house in a hollow log.
He was a fine big handsome fellow;
She was a beauty green and yellow;
He said that she was a wife most rare;
She said that he was beyond compare.
While as for their home in the hollow log,
It was just a palace, declared each frog.
And as for their baby why he
Was just a marvellous prodigy.
If he did but open his mouth and croak,
They laughed and thought it a splendid joke.
I tell you this story that you may see
How happy a frog and his wife may be.

[ROBERT MACK, FROM *WHEN ALL IS YOUNG*, 1888]

'He was a frog and she was a frog ...'

Croak! said the Toad, I'm hungry, I think,
Today I've had nothing to eat or to drink.
I'll crawl to the garden and jump through
    the pales,
And there I'll dine nicely on slugs and on
    snails;
Ho, ho! quoth the Frog, is that what you
    mean?
Then I'll hop away to the next meadow
    stream,
There I will drink and eat worms and slugs
    too
And then I shall have a good dinner like
    you.

[NURSERY RHYME, '"CROAK!" SAID THE TOAD']

What are little boys made of?
Frogs and snails and puppy-dogs tails.

[NURSERY RHYME]

FROGS AT SCHOOL I

The sun was shining softly,
The day was calm and cool,
When forty-five frog scholars met
Down by the shady pool.
Poor little frogs, like little folk,
Are always sent to school.

Their lessons seemed the strangest things:
They learned that grapes were sour;
They learned that four-and-twenty-days
Exactly make an hour;
That bricks were made of houses,
And corn was made of flour.

That six times one was ninety-five,
And 'yes' meant 'no' or 'nay';
They always spent tomorrow
Before they spent today;
While each commenced the alphabet
With Z instead of A.

As soon as school was over,
The master said: 'No noise!
Now go and play at leap-frog'
(The game a frog enjoys),
'And mind that you behave yourselves,
And don't throw stones at boys.'

[ANON]

66

FROGS AT SCHOOL II

Twenty froggies went to school
Down beside a rushy pool;
Twenty little coats of green,
Twenty vests all white and clean.

'We must be in time,' said they.
'First we study, then we play;
That is how we keep the rule,
When we froggies go to school.'

Master Bullfrog, grave and stern,
Called the classes in their turn;
Taught them how to nobly strive,
Likewise how to leap and dive.

From his seat upon a log,
Showed them how to say, 'Ker-chog!'
Also how to dodge a blow
From the sticks which bad boys throw.

Twenty froggies grew up fast;
Bullfrogs they became at last.
Not one dunce was in the lot,
Not one lesson they forgot.

Polished in a high degree,
As each froggy ought to be,
Now they sit on other logs,
Teaching other little frogs.

[GEORGE COOPER, (1840-1927)]

A little green frog once lived in a pool,
The sun was hot but the water was cool;
He sat in the pool the whole day long,
And sang a queer little, dear little song.

'Quaggery do, quaggery dee,
No one was ever so happy as me.'
He sang this song to his little green
   brother,
And if you don't like it then make me
   another.

[ROSE FYLEMAN, 'THE FROG']

Suzanna Frog is sleek and green,
Her eyes are staring, large and bold,
Around the water-hole, she's seen,
She lives there though 'tis rather cold.

The eggs she lays in one big heap,
Looks like boiled sago floating there,
And even if the water's deep,
Suzanna does not seem to care.

She leaves her eggs and hops away,
To find some insects for her tea,
She knows the eggs will hatch someday,
And so she does not wait to see.

On rainy days Suzanna sings,
That's when she's feeling glad and gay,
Her voice is harsh, but yet it brings,
A welcome note into the day.

[ISABEL FERRIS, 'SUZANNA FROG']

NONSENSE FROGS

There was an Old Person of Rhodes,
Who strongly objected to toads;
He paid several cousins, to catch them by
    dozens,
That futile Old Person of Rhodes.

[EDWARD LEAR, *A BOOK OF NONSENSE*, 1846]

There was an old man in a Marsh,
Whose manners were futile and harsh;
He sate on a log, and sang songs to a frog,
That instructive old man in a Marsh.

[EDWARD LEAR, *MORE NONSENSE*, 1872]

THE TONGUE-TWISTING ODE OF THE TWO-TOED TREE TOAD AND THE THREE-TOED TREE TOAD

A tree toad loved a she toad
That lived high in a tree.
She was a two-toed tree toad
But a three-toed toad was he.

The three-toed tree toad tried to win
The she-toad's nuptial nod;
For the three-toed tree toad loved the road
The two-toed tree toad trod.

Hard as the three-toed tree toad tried,
He could not reach her limb.
From her tree toad bower, with her V-toe
    power
The she toad vetoed him.

[ANON. FIRST PUBLISHED IN THE *MOBILE REGISTER*, ALABAMA, 12 AUGUST 1892]

The frog he sits upon the bank
And catches bugs and flies,
And after he gets tired of that
He just jumps in and dives.

[JAMES K. ELMORE 'THE FROG HE SITS']

What a wonderful bird the frog are —
When he stand he sit almost;
When he hop, he fly almost.
He ain't got no sense hardly;
He ain't got no tail hardly either.
When he sit, he sit on what he ain't got
    almost.

[ANON. FRENCH CANADIAN]

THEATRICAL FROGS

Aristophanes' satire, *The Frogs*, is probably the best-known theatrical manifestation of frogs — but it is not the only one. Lewis Carroll recorded in his diary that on 7 January 1875 he went to a pantomime called 'Froggy Would A-wooing Go' — '. . . one of the best pantomimes I ever saw'. 'Toad of Toad Hall' was A.A. Milne's stage adaptation of *Wind in the Willows*, first performed in 1930. It became a perennially popular show, performed every Christmas. The Muppet, Kermit the Frog, the 1975 creation of Jim Henson, has become perhaps the most famous frog character of all time through his television and cinema appearances.

MUSICAL FROGS

In Aristophanes' *The Frogs*, the frog chorus of 'Brekekekex coax coax' is repeated several times — perhaps the first dramatic attempt to imitate animal sounds. The chorus of frogs sings:

Brekekekex coax coax
Spawn of marsh and spring
Sing loud and sweet on a splendid
Theme set to the flute
coax coax

The Githawn or Salmon-Eater tribe of the Alaskan coast sing a so-called 'Frog Mourning Song' that relates to the punishment of young men for killing frogs.

A song that begins:
  'I went to a toad that lies under the well,
  I charmed him out, and he came at my
    call.'
appears as part of the song of a witch in Ben Jonson's *The Masque of Queens* (1609).

Thomas à Becket, a Dramatic Chronicle (1840) — a play by George Darley (1795-1846), features a song, 'Speckle-black Toad and freckle-green Frog':
Speckle-black Toad and freckle-green Frog,
Hopping together from quag to bog;
From pool to puddle
Right on they huddle;
Through thick and through thin,
Without tail or fin;
Croakle goes first and *Quackle* goes after,
Plash in the flood
And plump in the mud,
With slippery heels
Vaulting over eels,
And mouths to their middles split down
  with laughter!
Hu! hu! hex!

'A Frog He Would A-wooing Go', illustrated by Randolph Caldecott (1883).

A FROG HE WOULD A-WOOING GO
A frog he would a-wooing go,
Heigh ho! says Rowley,
A frog he would a-wooing go,
Whether his mother would let him or no.
With a rowley, powley, gammon and
    spinach,
Heigh-ho! says Anthony Rowley.

This is the relatively modern version of an old song. In *The Complaynt of Scotland* (1549) by an unknown author (perhaps Sir David Lyndsay) shepherds sing 'The frog cam to the myl dur,' and this is probably the same song as one dating from 1580, which was said to describe 'A most Strange weddinge of the

A frog minstrel promotes Tarrant's Seltzer in an advertisement of 1887.

ffrogge and the mouse'. In 1611, Thomas Ravenscroft's *Melismata* included the song of 'The Marriage of the Frogge and the Mouse' — a sad version in which, following the wedding feast, the mouse is caught by a cat and a duck carries the frog off. The well-known version was popularised in the nineteenth century by the clown Grimaldi and by the comedian, John Liston. In 1809 it was published with music as 'The Love-sick Frog,' and has since been widely adapted and parodied. King Charles II was known as 'Old

Going for a Gong — a bronze frog to summon guests to dinner.

Rowley,' and it has been suggested that he was the Rowley in the song — but as this line does not appear before the nineteenth century, the connection is unproven. The American song that begins:

'A frog went a-courting, and he did ride
Sword and pistol by his side'

Is very similar to:

There lived a Puddy [frog] in a well ...
Puddy he'd a-wooin ride
Sword and pistol by his side

which appears in K. Sharpe's *Ballad Book* (1824). Many variations of the British and American song have been recorded.

In Haydn's Quartet No: 49 in D Major, Opus 50 No. 6 (1785), a croaking frog is emulated by the strings — two violins, viola and violoncello.

Charles Thurber Miller (1830-76) produced his 'Frog Opera, with Pollywog Chorus,' the lyrics of which were published by Mudge and Co of Boston in 1872, when it was described as 'A burletta'. It must have achieved some success, as there were several later editions in which its origin and nature was further explained: 'A musical extravaganza founded on the nursery story of "A frog he would a-wooing go"'. A pollywog, in case you are wondering, is an American word for a tadpole!

In 1904, Kenneth Grahame (1859-1932) started telling his infant son Alastair (nicknamed 'Mouse') a story about '... moles, giraffes and water-rats'. This he continued in a series of letters, which developed into the book that was eventually published in 1908 as *The Wind in the Willows*. 'Toad of Toad Hall' has been regarded as the central character since the first dramatic performance. Beatrix Potter was actually critical of Grahame's portrayal of Mr Toad. In particular, she thought it absurd that he should be described as combing his hair — 'A mistake to fly in the face of nature,' she described it. 'A frog may wear galoshes; but I don't hold with toads having beards or wigs!' In one of his letters (17 July 1907) Grahame explained that Toad had:

... made up a song, in praise of himself, and sang it as he walked along and it *was* a conceited song! Here are some of the verses:—

> The world has held great Heroes,
> As history-books have showed;
> But never a name to go down to fame
> Compared with that of Toad!

> The clever men at Oxford
> Know all that there is to be knowed.
> But they none of them know one half as much
> As intelligent Mr Toad!

Arthur Rackham's illustration of Mr Toad's escape from prison in The Wind in the Willows. *The jailer's kindly daughter disguises him as her aunt, a washerwoman, telling him, 'You're the very image of her!'*

> The animals sat in the Ark and cried,
> Their tears in torrents flowed.
> Who was it said, 'There's land ahead'?
> Encouraging Mr Toad!

> The Army all saluted
> As they marched along the road.
> Was it the King? Or Kitchener?
> No. It was Mr Toad.

> The Queen and her Ladies-in-waiting
> Sat at the window and sewed.
> She cried, 'Look! who's that *handsome* man?'
> They answered, 'Mr Toad.'

Coming full circle to Aristophenes' frog chorus, a 'Frog Chorus' appears in Paul McCartney's award-winning cartoon film, *Rupert and the Frog Song* (1984).

THE FROG IN ART

Roman mosaics are among the earliest artistic manifestations of frogs. Frogs appear occasionally in Medieval manuscript miniatures — especially in representations of the Biblical plague of frogs — and in bestiaries (catalogues of real and fabulous animals). The frog appears only rarely in fine art, and when it does it usually performs some symbolic role, such as in Hieronymus Bosch's *Temptation of St. Anthony* in which a frog has the head of an aged person. The illustration of printed books, however, has produced a number of splendid portrayals of frogs:

NATURAL HISTORY ILLUSTRATORS

Of all natural history illustrators who have depicted frogs, among the greatest is Mark Catesby (c1679-1749). His frogs, shown in their natural habitat in his *The Natural History of Carolina, Florida and the Bahama*

Above: Toad in a Landscape — a 19th-century watercolour by Aloys Zötls.

Left: an 1835 illustration of a toad with his family album.

Islands (1731-43), are outstandingly beautiful. Similarly excellent are the frog pictures of Augustin Johann Roesel Von Rosenhof whose *Historia Naturalis Ranarum Nostratium*, published in Nuremberg in 1758, contains detailed scientific illustrations of frogs headed by a magnificent frontispiece in which frogs and lizards cavort amid luxuriant foliage. Among other natural history and scientific illustrators are F.M. Daudin's *Histoire Naturelle des Rainettes, des Grenouilles et des Crapauds [Natural History of Tree Frogs, Frogs and Toads]* (Paris: 1802-03), which contains thirty-eight colour plates,

Frog-catching, medieval style, from a book of poems by Christine de Pesan.

Frogs and their relatives from Roesel Von Rosenhof's Historia Naturalis *(1758).*

Tree frog from Daudin's Histoire Naturelle.

some of which are rather imaginatively drawn, despite the declaration that they were 'painted from nature'.

'J.J. GRANDVILLE'

Jean-Ignace-Isidore Gérard (1803-47), a French artist who worked under the name, 'J.J. Grandville,' was a notable caricaturist who contributed to such humorous magazines as *Charivari*. He also illustrated a number of books in which he characteristically depicted people as animals, scathingly satirizing human vices and the personalities of his subjects. Grandville was particularly fascinated by frogs, and even kept one in his

A perfect gentleman frog, one of many by frog enthusiast, J.J. Grandville.

apartment at 26 rue des Saints-Pères in Paris. During the summer, he took time off from his drawing to go down to his garden every day to catch insects on a sunny wall for his pet frog's lunch. One of his biographers describes how once, while staying at Nancy, Grandville was busily sketching a basketful of frogs, '... eager and intent, exactly noting down reality, striving for unerring correction of line and typical expressions'. As he drew, however, so absorbed did he become with his work that he lost all track of time and failed to notice that the frogs were steadily escaping from their basket and invading the entire house! Grandville is perhaps best known for his major work, *The Public and Private Life of Animals*, published in France in 1842 and in England in 1877 — in which, of course, frogs feature prominently. There are also various 'frog people' in his *Metamorphoses du Jour* (1828).

JOHN TENNIEL

Grandville's bizarre animals have been seen by some as the inspiration behind many of John Tenniel's famous illustrations for Lewis Carroll's *Alice in Wonderland* — and indeed, a 'frog footman' drawn by Grandville is remarkably similar to the one that appears in *Alice*.

EDWARD LEAR

Edward Lear started his artistic career as a natural history painter, and later frequently found comic potential in frogs and toads: limericks such as his 'Old Person of Rhodes'

and his 'Old Man in a Marsh' featured them, as did his 'A Visit from Two Considerate Frogs,' an illustrated letter he wrote to Lady Duncan on 7 January 1865.

BEATRIX POTTER

In her journal, which she wrote in her own secret code, Beatrix Potter recorded a visit to St. Albans when she was seventeen, and her exploits with frogs in a local pond. She also kept a pet frog, and on 19 March 1884 she noted, 'Poor little *Punch* died on the 11th., green frog, had him five or six years. He has been on extensive journeys.' In 1892, she showed some frog drawings to a German printing firm called Nisters; they rather enig-matically told her that 'people do not want frogs now,' but after protracted negotiations, she sold them for 22/6d for reproduction in a children's annual under the title, 'A Frog He Would a-Fishing Go'.

The first of Beatrix Potter's famous books started out as illustrated letters to Noël and Annie Moore, the children of one of her former governesses. *The Tale of Mr Jeremy Fisher* was just such a story, which began life partly as a letter she wrote to them in 1893 and partly as her Nisters' frog pictures, which she bought back from them for £6. It was published in 1906 and was a great success — and the ballet solo depicting Jeremy is one of the most memorable in the film, *The Tales of Beatrix Potter*.

Frogs and toads continued to be favourites of Potter's. As well as *Punch* she kept a toad,

'Caught in the Act' and 'Avenger of His Honour' — a frog drama depicted in his Sketchbook II *by the 19th-century German satirical illustrator, Heinrich Kley.*

whose feeding habits she closely observed — Mr Jackson, a greedy toad, accordingly appears in *The Tale of Mrs Tittlemouse* (1910).

OTHER ILLUSTRATORS

Various Victorian and Edwardian illustrators, among them Heinrich Kley and Ernest Henry Griset, working in a caricature style found inspiration in frogs. Randolph Caldecott (1846-86) illustrated a superb version of *A Frog He Would A-wooing Go* in 1883 (the original illustrations are in the Victoria & Albert Museum). Walter Crane (1845-1915), one of the most popular children's book illustrators of the late nineteenth century, often drew frogs: they appear in his *A Gaping Wide-mouth Waddling Frog* (1866), *Butterfly's Ball* and in his popular version of the Brothers Grimm's fairy tale, *The Frog Prince* (1901). 'BTB' (Basil Temple Blackwood, 1870-1917) provided the illustrations for Hilaire Belloc's *The Bad Child's Book of Beasts* (1896), which included one of a large frog sitting on a table. Milicent Sowerby, who illustrated *The Frog Prince* in 1909, was one of many who produced pictures to accompany Grimm's *Fairy Tales*. Arthur Rackham's illustrations for Aesop's *Fables* and Grimm, as well as *The Wind in the Willows*, all contain frogs and toads, though Ernest Shepard's pictures of Mr Toad for the 1931 edition of *The Wind in the Willows* are perhaps the best known. Numerous other illustrators have tackled the depiction of Toad — although it is known that Kenneth Grahame himself was opposed to the idea of attempting to illustrate his book. The Australian children's book illustrator, Ida Rentoul Outhwaite, published a number of elaborate works in the period 1900-35. The pictures in her book, *Fairyland* (1926) contain, in addition to fairies, her two favourite animals: koala bears (giving her version of fairyland a distinctly Antipodean ambiance) and frogs, which appear in almost every scene, from a regatta to a fairy wedding — in which the vicar is a frog! Mervyn Peake provided illustrations for Christina Hole's *Witchcraft in England* (1945), in which he included a witch with her toad familiar.

HERALDIC FROGS

In the church at Bainton, Yorkshire, there is a recumbent effigy of a thirteenth-century knight. A toad covers the point of his sword, perhaps symbolising the similarly lethal nature of the weapon and of toad venom. A gold frog is oddly attached to the ear of the effigy of Sir John Poley at Boxted church,

Frogs in the lily pond — a woodcut by Dutch artist Maurits Cornelis Escher (1898-1972).

The princess and the as-yet unkissed Frog Prince, by Arthur Rackham (1900).

Left:
'My, how you've changed!' Walter Crane's illustration to The Frog Prince *(1901).*

Above:
One of Arthur Rackham's drawings for Aesop's 'The Ox and the Frog' (1912).

Suffolk, and appears in a portrait of him. This possibly derives from his membership of the 'Knights of the Elephant,' a Danish chivalric order which also used a frog emblem. Frogs and toads occasionally appear in coats of arms, such as that of Botereux of Cornwall, which is described as 'three toads erected sable'.

HOW MUCH IS THAT FROGGY IN THE WINDOW?

As a visit to any gift shop will show, frogs are among the most popular animals, every conceivable collectable object appearing in their form. Once hooked, frog-lovers seem to find them irresistible: Princess Diana is reputed to have a substantial collection, including her frog car mascot, given by Prince Andrew; echoes of the Frog Prince, perhaps? Actress Wendy Richards also has a collection of froggy objects. A Mrs Mabel Winters and her family, of Fort Smith Arkansas, are perhaps the world's leading frog collectors; their collection of several thousand frog artefacts, pictures and books includes frogs made out of precious metals, rubber, ceramics, volcanic ash, tallow, straw, jade, ivory and sugar; over 600 of them are from Mexico alone. Her collection began in Mexico in 1936 when she obtained a small plastic frog from a chewing gum machine — so be warned, the disease is easily caught!

Your frog collection might even include archaeological treasures such as Egyptian frog amulets, garden ornaments and Japanese netsuke (ivory or wooden belt toggles, often carved in the shape of tiny animals). Jewelled frogs are not unknown: such famous craftsmen as Carl Fabergé in Russia and Tiffany in New York made frogs in gold and precious stones.

Equally desirable, but unobtainable, frogs include the British Museum's nineteenth-century Red Indian wooden feast bowl from Haida in the Queen Charlotte Islands, British Columbia, skilfully carved in the shape of a

'A Regatta', with frog Water Police, by Australian illustrator Ida Outhwaite.

frog, and inn signs such as those depicting the 'Frog and Firkin' and the rather strangely named 'Frog and Nightgown' in London's Old Kent Road. A grotesque stuffed frog with an umbrella was exhibited as part of a taxidermy display at the Great Exhibition in 1851 with the title, 'The Morning Walk'.

Frog toys, including wind-up clockwork toys, Victorian games and money boxes, were once enormously popular: a substantial collection of these and other ornamental frogs can be seen in the Dolls House Toy Museum in Arundel, Sussex. 'Frogger,' a computer game, is the 1980s' high-tech tribute to frogs.

I have hopped, when properly wound up, the whole length
Of the hallway; once hopped halfway down the stairs, and fell,

Since then the two halves of my tin have been awry; my strength
Is not quite what it used to be; I do not hop so well.

[RUSSELL HOBAN, 'THE TIN FROG,' FROM *THE PEDALLING MAN AND OTHER POEMS*, 1968]

THE FROG IN PRINT

Collectors might add to their range of 'frogiana' such items as postcards, advertisements and sheet music covers featuring frogs. The frog has also been a popular subject for caricature: the frog as a symbol of a Frenchman was used in various satirical prints — one of 1829, titled 'The Frog and the Bull,' depicts the Duke of Wellington as the bull with the French Foreign Minister, Prince Jules de Polignac, as the frog. Cartoons of frog princes and other frog subjects are commonly found: one of them, Sam Gross'

An imposing New Zealand frog, skilfully carved from a bamboo root.

A Victorian frog money box — a lever causes him to flip coins into his mouth.

KERR & Cᵒˢ ÆSOP'S FABLES

The FROGS asking for a KING. (see other side)

EXTRA SIX CORD SPOOL COTTON.

Above: Aesop's Fables *bizarrely adapted to advertise reels of cotton.*

Above right: Croaky throats guaranteed by nautical tobacco-advertising frogs.

cartoon of a double amputee frog was made famous by the American satirical magazine, *National Lampoon*, which reproduced it as a 'designer' motif to replace that most 'preppy' logo, the Lacoste alligator. In 1983, Don Dougherty, an American cartoonist, even published a whole book of frog cartoons, *Croakers*.

FROG POTS

Sculpture featuring frogs is not unknown, and includes spouting frog fountains, Mexican stone carvings and Peruvian frog tomb statuettes and bowls decorated with frogs and tadpoles. Lamps in the shape of a frog decorated with early Christian slogans have been found.

'Sunderland Frog Mugs' were popular in the nineteenth century. They are ceramic drinking mugs with frogs or toads at the bottom, made so that they blow bubbles in the beer, and make a gurgling sound when tipped. When the drinker hears the noise and sees the frog, he is often so surprised that he

A mouse-drawn carriage carries frogs to the Epsom Derby in a work dating from c1886 by Doulton potter George Tinworth.

'The Voice from the Swamp' — an anti-Nazi photomontage by John Heartfield, first published in AIZ *(19 March 1936).*

drops the mug and smashes it — and they are hence rather rare! Sometimes there was a warning rhyme on the side:

Though malt and venom seem united,
Don't break my pot or be affrighted.

A less common version of this was made in the form of a chamber pot.

George Tinworth (1843-1913) worked as a potter with the Doulton company from 1866. His religious subjects were much praised by the art critic, John Ruskin, but as though needing some comic diversion from them, he often turned to creating glazed stoneware depicting animals, and frogs were his favourites: his 'Steeplechase' (c1875) portrays a frantic gallop of frogs astride mice as they leap a hurdle — some falling and scrabbling in the ditch. Frogs riding mice do battle with spears in a work from about the same year, while pieces dating from c1880 show a frog playing cricket and riding a penny-farthing bicycle. In c1885 Tinworth's 'Art and Agricul-

The Frog in the Pot: a rare Victorian frog chamber pot — traditionally given as a gift from husband to wife —   which when emptied, makes an alarming gurgling noise.

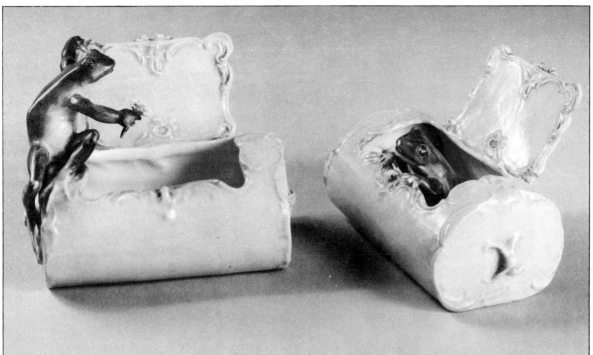

A decorative frog — would a-wooing go . . .

ture — Albert Embankment' presented two frogs seated on a Thames Embankment bench; one poses with a basket of fruit, while the other works on a picture of his companion. In c1886 he returned to his 'equestrian' frogs with 'Going to the Derby' — a lively scene of frogs in an open carriage drawn by a mouse; a sign reads 'To Epsom'. So famous did Tinworth become through his often bizarre frog-inspired works, that Tinworth Street, near Doulton's Lambeth factory, was named in his honour.

A contemporary potter, Anthony Bennett, has perpetuated the tradition of manufacturing stoneware frogs and jugs depicting brightly coloured frogs in human shapes.

FROGS' LEGS AND TOAD-IN-THE-HOLE: A SHORT GUIDE TO FROG CUISINE

'I marvel why frogs and snails are with some people, and in some countries, in great account, and judged wholesome food, whereas indeed they have in them nothing else but a cold, gross, slimy and excremental juice.'

[TOBIAS VENNER, *VIA RECTA*, 1620]

'I have been in France, and have eaten frogs. The nicest little rabbity things you ever tasted. Make Mrs Clare pick off the hind quarters, boil them plain, with parsley and butter. The fore quarters are not so good. She may let them hop off by themselves.'

[CHARLES LAMB, LETTER TO JOHN CLAIRE, 31 AUGUST 1822]

The Green (edible) frog, *Rana esculenta*, is a native of Europe and parts of Asia and North Africa, but in France, frogs were not regarded as a gourmet delicacy until the sixteenth century, and in the nineteenth century Vienna was also thought of as a leading frog-eating city. The Catholic church regards frogs as fish rather than meat; hence in Catholic countries it is permitted to eat them on meat-less days — which also explains why they appear in the 'Fish' section of French menus.

Eating frogs' legs has often been greeted with distaste: the great chef, Escoffier, used the euphemism, 'nymphs,' in his frog recipes, and there are many descriptions of foreigners' encounters with frogs, such as that of

Culinary frogs consult their cookbook.

An edible frog jumping for its life.

naturalist Frank Buckland in his *Curiosities of Natural History* (1857) — published when 'foreign' food was regarded with suspicion:

In France, frogs are considered a luxury, as any *bon vivant* ordering a dish of them at the *Trois Frères*, at Paris, may, by the long price, speedily ascertain. Not wishing to try such an expensive experiment in gastronomy, I went to the large market in the Faubourg St Germain, and enquired for frogs. I was referred to a stately-looking dame at a fish-stall, who produced a box nearly full of them, huddling and crawling about, and occasionally croaking as though aware of the fate to which they were destined. The price fixed was two a penny, and having ordered a dish to be prepared, the *Dame de la Halle* dived her hand in among them, and having secured her victim by the hind legs, she severed him in twain with a sharp knife; the legs, minus skin, still struggling, were placed on a dish; and the head, with the fore-legs affixed, retained life and motion, and performed such motions that the operation became painful to look at. The legs were afterwards cooked at the *restaurateur's*, being served up fried in bread crumbs, as larks are in England; and most excellent eating they were, tasting more like the delicate flesh of the rabbit than anything else I can think of. I afterwards tried a dish of the common English frog, but his flesh is not so white nor so tender as that of his French brother.

Outside France, frog recipes occur throughout the world: curried Manila frog is described by nineteenth-century travel writer MacMicking in his *Manila*. Alfred Russel Wallace (1823-1913), in his *Travels on the Amazon and Rio Negro* (1853), describes catching and eating frogs called *jui*. Giant frogs are eaten in Dominica; soup made from them was regarded as especially good for consumptives. In the United States of America the bullfrog (*Rana catesbeiana*) is the principal type eaten; up to eight inches long, it is mainly found in the Eastern States. *Rana areolata*, the 'gopher frog,' is eaten in the Midwest and is half the size of a bullfrog. *Rana clamitans*, the green frog, which is about four inches long, is eaten in the east, Midwest and south, *Rana palustris*, the pickerel frog, up to three inches long, is also eaten.

DR BROEL'S 'FAMOUS WAYS TO SERVE GIANT FROG'

In his comprehensive manual on frog-farming and cooking, *Frog Raising for Pleasure and Profit* (1950) (see also pages 23-25), Dr Albert Broel provides this unique list of over fifty tempting recipes for Giant Frogs:

Giant Frog Gumbo
Fried Frog Legs
Giant Frog Sandwich Spread
Fricassee of Giant Bullfrog
French Fried Giant Frog and Soup Colbert
Giant Bullfrog Cream Broth

Devilled Giant Bullfrog Meat
American Giant Bullfrog Cocktail
American Giant Bullfrog Pie, Country Style
Giant Bullfrog Mince Meat
Giant Bullfrogs Jellied
Giant Bullfrog Club House Sandwich
Giant Bullfrog Croquettes
Giant Bullfrog Meat with Dumplings
Grilled Giant Bullfrog Sandwich
Barbecued Giant Bullfrog Sandwiches
Giant Bullfrog Dressing
Giant Bullfrog Meat and Rice, Chinese
    Style
Giant Bullfrog Chop Suey
Jellied Giant Bullfrog Creamed Salad
Giant Bullfrog Salad
Dominant Mayonnaise Dressing for Giant
    Frogs
Giant Bullfrog Luncheon with Tomatoes
Giant Bullfrog Luncheon with Corn
Escalloped Giant Bullfrog with Celery and
    Potatoes
Giant Bullfrog à la King
Giant Bullfrog Pot Pie
Minced Giant Bullfrog Savory Sandwiches
Hot Giant Bullfrog Sandwiches with
    Newberg Sauce
Giant Bullfrog Meat Russian Sandwich
Giant Bullfrog Short Cakes
Giant Bullfrog Sandwich Loaf
Giant Bullfrog Pineapple Salad
Creamed Giant Bullfrog and Mushrooms
Giant Bullfrog Omelet
Baked Apples stuffed with Giant Frog
    Meat

Stuffed Egg with Giant Bullfrog
Stuffed Baked Tomatoes with Giant
    Bullfrogs
Giant Bullfrog Meat with Asparagus
Giant Bullfrog au Gratin
Giant Bullfrog Legs Italian
Giant Bullfrog Paprikosh
Giant Bullfrog Maryland
Giant Bullfrog Meat with Devilled Ham
    Sandwich
Hot Diced Giant Bullfrog Meat (canned)
    and Devilled Ham
Giant Bullfrog Meat, Currant Jelly and
    Cottage Cheese
Giant Bullfrog Three Layer Sandwich
Giant Bullfrog Charlotte
Giant Bullfrog Fondue
Giant Bullfrog Meat June Salad
French Toasted Giant Bullfrog Meat Special

If this doesn't put you off, a final word on the international trade in frogs' legs. This huge market is led by India, Bangladesh, Indonesia, Laos and Vietnam who export to Europe, the United States, Canada and Japan. There is, however, a current movement against this traffic on grounds of hygiene, cruelty and ecology: there are obvious problems caused by removing frogs from the ecosystem, since the insects they would otherwise eat have to be dealt with through the increased use of pesticides. The West German anti-frog movement, 'lasst den Froscen ihre schenkel' — let the frogs keep their legs — is likely to be the slogan of the future.

A FROG IN THE THROAT: FROG WORDS AND PHRASES

SOME OBSCURE FROG WORDS

amplexus — the sexual embrace of amphibians, such as frogs and toads.

apron — the fold of skin on the throat of some toads.

batrachian — relating to frogs and toads.

batrachite — a stone or gem that resembles a frog.

boiling school — when tadpoles of *Scaphiopus*, the American Spadefoot toad, rush up to the surface of a pond and plunge down again to disturb the mud and find food.

bufo-chrome — not a new type of metal polish, but fluorescent chemicals found in the skin of *Bufo vulgaris*.

bufonite — a fossilised 'toadstone'.

critical tadpole — A frog larva whose development is arrested through lack of nourishment — well, wouldn't you be critical?

croaker — a frog, as in Aesop's *Fables*: 'While the long Vale with deep-voiced Croakers rings.'

Dutch nightingale — a frog.

frog — a policeman who, froglike, leaps upon a criminal.
— a foot.
— a disease of the throat.
— part of a horse's hoof.
— the hollow in a brick.
— part of a plough.
— a tamper used in road construction.
— a dishonoured or 'bouncing' cheque.
— part of a railway track.
— part of a violin bow.
— Australian slang for a £1 note (supposedly from rhyming 'frogskin' with 'sovrin', or sovereign).

frog/froggy — a derogatory term used in computer jargon.

frog action — bicycle polo.

frog and toad — rhyming slang for 'road'.

frog and toe — slang term for London.

frog('s)-bit — an aquatic plant.

frog-crab — a *Ranina* crab.

frog-dance — a hornpipe-like dance.

frog-eye — a disease of tobacco.

frog-footed/footer — on foot.

froggery — a gathering of frogs.

frogging — ornamentation on a coat.

froggy — American black slang for aggressively eager to fight.

frog hair — money used corruptly in a political campaign (disguised, and hence as invisible as frog hair); also the grass between a fairway and a green on a golf course.

Frog Hall — an East Anglian expression for a small house with a pretentiously large garden.

froghood — quality or standing as a frog.

frog-hopper — an insect.

frog in the throat — Cockney rhyming slang for boat.

frog it — to walk or march.

froglander — a Dutchman. In John Arbuthnot's *Law is a Bottomless Pit* (1712), a Dutchman is called 'Nic Frog'. Arbuthnot was physician to Queen Anne, and a noted satirist.

frogling — a small frog.

frog or **frog's march** — to carry a prisoner face down by his arms and legs — so he is spread out like a frog

frog-pecker — a heron.

Frogpondian — an inhabitant of Boston, Mass.

frog position — a froglike stance adopted by a parachutist.

frog's mouth — the snapdragon.

frog's wine — gin.

frogs' eyes/spawn — slang term for tapioca.

Galli-Mainini Test — a pregnancy test using *Rana pipiens* or other frogs.

grenouillière — A 'froggery,' or place where frogs are fattened for consumption.

hallux — the first innermost toe of the hind foot of a frog or toad.

herp — a slang term for reptiles and amphibians in general.

herpesian — pertaining to reptiles and amphibians.

herpetography — writing about frogs, toads and other reptiles and amphibians.

herpetomy — dissecting frogs, toads and other reptiles and amphibians.

loggerhead — a tadpole.

imago — the stage immediately after the metamorphosis of a frog or toad.

leapfrog — a term used in industrial relations, referring to repeated overtaking in wage claims.

og-fray — pig latin for frog (in the sense of Frenchman).

paddock, poddock, puddock, etc — an archaic word for a frog or toad.

polliwog, pollywog, porriwiggle, etc — originally British, but now more commonly an American term for a type of tadpole.

rana-chrome — like bufo-chrome — a fluorescent chemical found in the skin of *Rana nigromaculata*.

ranarium — a place where frogs are kept; a frog farm.

ranid — belonging to the frog family.

ranine — pertaining to frogs.

ranivorous — frog-eating.

rasping organ — the horny teeth of frog tadpoles.

red leg — a bacterial disease of frogs.

skitter — rapid skimming movement over the surface of water found among certain Asiatic frogs.

tad — short for tadpole.

tadpoledom, tadpolehood, tadpolism — the state of being a tadpole.

tick — a sound like a watch being wound — the female *Xenophus* makes it if clasped by a male before she is ready to spawn.

toad — toast dunked in beer

— a kind of German hand-grenade used in the First World War.
— a popular malefactor (Marlborough College slang).
— Canadian railroad slang for a derailer.
— a type of Dutch fishing boat.

toadery — a place where toads are kept.

toadflax — a *Linaria* plant.

toadlet — a newly-metamorphosed toad.

toadling — a small toad.

THE PROVERBIAL FROG — FROG PHRASES AND PROVERBS

An April flood carries away the frog and her brood.

As free from feathers as a frog.

As full of money as a toad is of feathers.

As much as a toad needs side-pockets.

As pert as a frog on a washing block.

To catch a frog (to gain little after great exertions).

Fish fair and catch a frog.

Fond fisher that angles for a frog.

A frog in a well knows nothing of the high seas. [Japanese proverb]

Frog (or toad) said to the harrow, the cursed be so many lords.

The frog's own croak betrays him.

Gossips are frogs, they drink and talk.

His purse is made of a toad's skin.

Like a toad under a harrow.

Look to him, jailer, there's a frog in the stocks.

Naked as a frog.

Sit like a frog (or toad) on a chopping-block.

Smell like a toad.

The frog cannot out of her bog (the same sense as 'A leopard can't change its spots').

To hate one like a toad.

When a frog flies into a passion, the pond knows nothing of it. [Greek proverb]

FROGRAPHY

A number of British place-names are derived from frog connections. They include Frognal, from 'Frogen-hall' — the Saxon word, *frogen*, means frogs; Frogmore; Frog Hall — examples existed near Kineton, Dunsmoor Heath, Ramsay, Cheadle, Wokingham and Halstead. There are also various Frog Groves, Frog Hills, Frog Moors, Froggatts and Frog Lanes. Frog Lane in London, which once ran from Finsbury Fields to Newington Green, had just one house — called Frog Hall.

FROG ORGANIZATIONS

Association for the Study of Reptilia and Amphibia
The ASRA Rooms
Cotswold Wildlife Park
Burford, Oxon
OX8 4JW
Tel: 099 382 3006
[Publish *Rephiberary*]

British Herpetological Society
c/o Zoological Society of London
Regent's Park
London NW1 4RY
[Publish the *British Journal of Herpetology*]

The American Society of Ichthyologists and Herpetologists
Department of Ichthyology
American Museum of Natural History
New York
New York 10024
Tel: (212) 873 1279

The Herpetologists' League
8515 Youree Drive
Louisiana State University
Department of Biological Sciences
Shreveport
L.A. 71115
Tel: (318) 491 5376

THE FROG LIBRARY

A selective bibliography of the dozen best frog books.

E.N. Arnold and J.A. Burton
A Field Guide to the Reptiles and Amphibians of Britain and Europe
London, 1980
[An excellent pictorial summary]

Trevor Beebee
Frogs and Toads
London, 1985
[A first rate introduction to the subject]

Arthur Bragg
Gnomes of the Night: the Spadefoot Toads
Philadelphia, 1965
[The best book on this little-known species]

Albert Broel
Frog Raising for Pleasure and Profit
New Orleans, 1950
[An undeliberately hilarious book on frog farming; a facsimile of an earlier, shorter edition was published in 1985]

Doris M. Cochran
Living Amphibians of the World
London, 1961
[A superbly illustrated and readable survey]

Mary Cynthia Dickerson
The Frog Book
New York, 1906
[An excellent, but rare book on American frogs and toads]

Gerald Donaldson
Frogs
Leicester, 1980
[A super illustrated anthology]

Deryk Frazer
Reptiles and Amphibians in Britain
London, 1983
[A thorough factual survey]

Lynn Hughes
Frogs
London, 1982
[A tiny but interesting anthology of froggy writings]

Alfred Leutscher
Keeping Reptiles and Amphibians
Newton Abbott, 1976
[Everything you ever need to know about the subject]

Linda Sonntag
Frogs
London, 1981
[A small, beautifully designed gift book for frog-lovers]

Graham Tarrant
Frogs
New York, 1983
[The one and only pop-up (hop-up?) frog book]